# Chapter 1

# What is Brand Licensing?

Do you want to build your brand licensing dynasty, but are uncertain on the processes to take to guide your brand in this direction? Don't worry. With this Brand Licensing eBook, the process has been broken down into specific chapters that address specific questions to enable you, the brand owner, to grow your business with simplicity and understanding. As you progress through this guidebook you will notice that the terms (*brand owner* and *licensor*) and (*licensee* and *manufacturer*) are used interchangeably. In this first chapter the focus will be directed toward a frequently asked question, what is brand licensing? For context, we will focus on the origins of brand licensing, and why companies choose to license. The goal is that once finished with this chapter of Breakthrough Licensing, you will have the knowledge of what brand licensing is.

\*\*\*

Before discussing what brand licensing is, one must first understand what a brand is. According to Philip Kotler and Gary Armstrong, a brand is defined as "a name, term, sign, symbol or combination of these, that identifies the maker or seller of the product or service."[2] The brand affixed to the product helps the consumer understand where it was manufactured or produced. From the brand owner's perspective, it distinguishes the products or services from those of its competitors. Consumers, in turn, can be assured the product they are purchasing is exactly what they want. Based on its reputation, a brand will convey a level of quality, reliability, and durability.

In understanding the formality of a brand, try to imagine one of your own personal relationships. In referencing your relationship, you first build awareness with the person, then you introduce that person to close family and friends, next you start to build trust with that person which involves getting to understand what you prefer about them and what they prefer about you. With a brand, it is very similar. The relationship starts where the brand hears what you are saying while also making sure that they are continually delivering on a promise they've made to you. Once the relationship with the brand is developed, you increase the number of purchases made based on the commitments they make, the consistency of these commitments, and the way they make you feel. Brands also lead consumers to develop certain expectations of products. The longer you experience predictable quality and consistent performance, the more you rightfully will grow to expect any new products sold under the same brand to have the same qualities and attributes.

Let's take a moment to look at a couple of big brands and why they make a difference starting with the Nike swoosh. When looking at the Nike swoosh, it evokes a lot of feelings and attributes that would be considered important to a brand such as reliability, performance, and comfort. Nike has earned the trust of many consumers and has become a brand that is respected and used in people's day-to-day lives. The relationship that Nike has built over time delivers and outperforms that of many other manufacturers of athletic apparel. Many people are aware of the Nike brand. Nike's strong presence is an essential part of why Nike is a brand and why other manufacturers of athletic apparel aren't in the same classification as Nike. Nike understands that building a relationship is a crucial component, and without it, a brand can continue to remain a mystery.

*Nike Swoosh Symbol;*
*Source: Nike Website*

Another well-known brand is Meghan Markle; a former actress turned Duchess of Sussex. Now, I know what you're thinking. Can a person be a brand? The answer is simply, yes. Anyone can be a brand as long as they can identify what they stand for and communicate that promise with their audience on a personal level that evokes feeling. Since Meghan's engagement, and now marriage to Prince Harry, each brand of clothing she wears is intensively reviewed by publications around the globe. This worldwide coverage has sparked tremendous interest in the Meghan Markle brand. Many brands that she has worn thus far have experienced a boost in sales and an increase in global recognition. The key to this licensing success is that Markle has chosen brands that coincide with her brand position. She has not entered into categories that disrupt the relationships she has already developed. Meghan Markle wasn't recognized as a brand solely because of her acting abilities or because she married Prince Harry. She created relationships with people that formed strong bonds that made her fans want more of her. In a sense, Meghan Markle as a brand has become addictive, which suggests that her brand has bankability enabling the relationships themselves to be managed proactively to keep customers constantly looking out for new opportunities to engage. Consider the Gucci, Lexus, and John Deere brands. Even if you have never owned one of these brands, you

*The Duchess of Sussex at The Prince of Wales' 70th Birthday Patronage Celebration; Source: Time Rooke/REX/SHUTTERSTOCK*

have more than likely been exposed to them through a variety of outlets such as in-store and online retailers, mass commercial broadcast, or magazines. Each brand has its own products, services, and expectations that differentiate it from its competitors. Gucci has built a reputation and level of addictiveness that has caused customers to fall in love with the brand. John Deere's tagline: Nothing runs like a deer, conveys their enduring commitment to their customers. Lexus has been ranked number one in quality and performance by J.D. Power for decades and it's incredible what they've done with Lexus since their origins in the late 80's early 90's. All three are examples of successful brands.

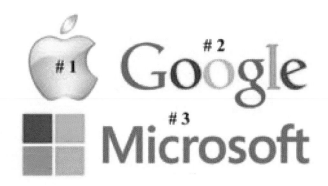

*Top Three Brands in the World*

According to Forbes, the 2018 top three brands in the world today based on brand value are Apple ($170B), Google ($101.8B), and Microsoft ($87B); these probably comes as no surprise.1 Although, what is surprising is that Coca-Cola is not on the top three list. Coca-Cola has traditionally ranked N° 1 or N° 2, but unfortunately, with the success of other brands increasing, they have dropped to N° 6. However, in the future, Coca-Cola will more than likely work its way back up to one of the top three slots. Reflecting on the top three brands, no one is doing better than Apple which is leading the pack at N° 1 in the world and N° 1 in market value for the company.[6] Google is also doing exceptionally well, due to top of mind awareness when an Internet search needs to be done. Although Google is much more than that; it's on mobile devices; it's a way to analyze the website, and it's an email platform. All of which has resulted in Google becoming the N° 2 brand in the world. So, with the consistent changes and new innovative ways Google has created for users, Google is constantly adding value to the brand, making the brand what it is today. The N° 3 spot is claimed by Microsoft who is an American technology company that operates on a multinational platform. Microsoft has been around for decades, but they still are finding new and creative ways to reinvent themselves to add more value to the brand. Microsoft is phenomenally successful and probably will continue to be for decades further.

*Figure 1-1 Different Types of Brand Licensing*

There are different types of brand licensing that are normally seen. The first is Corporate Licensing, which includes corporate brands like Amazon, Walt Disney, and Coca-Cola. **Corporate Licensing** helps corporate brands expand into new territories that could have been impossible to infiltrate without licensing programs, which enable the brand to stay true to the idea for which they are renowned. An example of this is Coca-Cola partnering with the Nagano Olympic Committee (co-licensor), Aminco, a pin company, and other licensees to produce Coca- Cola Nagano Olympic trading pins, apparel, plush, and commemorative bottles to sell. Without licensing with the Nagano Olympic Committee and the program licensees the opportunity to expand the brand in this area and sell millions of dollars of merchandise likely would have been lost.

The second type of licensing that is normally seen is **Character Licensing**. At the 2017 International Licensing Expo in Las Vegas, Character licensing was a dominant topic at the show. In attendance were Disney, Marvel, and Warner Brothers which own some of the most highly sought-after character brands we traditionally think about when we think of Character Licensing. It is these character brands that consumers know and want on a variety of cherished products. Character brands are extremely popular which has enticed businesses to want these brands on their products. Licensing with character brands helps businesses connect with the consumers and grab that associative imagery of those characters to make their brands more exciting.

The third type of licensing is **Fashion Licensing**. Versace is an international luxury Italian fashion company that began by serving a female target. As Gianni Versace's popularity increased, so did his brand and the demand for his designs. With the growth of the organization, the brand was able to extend into men's clothing, and not long after, Versace expanded into accessories, jewelry, fragrance, home furnishings, dining and much more. Even though they started out targeting a select market, the opportunity to enter other categories became inevitable. For the brand to grow the owner chose to extend via licensing enabling it to develop a powerful connection with consumers. Extending a fashion brand out of its core category into new categories, while also staying true to its expansion point, encourages consumers to consider the brand in other categories.

The next type of licensing is **Technology Licensing**. This includes Apple, Google, and Microsoft and also a slew of other brands that fall into the technology category such as PlayStation and iPhone. For instance, if Apple were to license with a type of food brand like Smuckers, it would not make as much sense as it would if Apple licensed with another kind of technology brand such as Beats.

**Art Licensing** is another type of licensing, which is increasingly growing. Technology is continually changing, and the digital era is becoming more prominent in everyone's lives. Due to technological advancements, more companies can now take advantage of the thousands of pieces of art created by artists each year. These pieces are digitized and made available through Art Licensing to make their brand and products more desirable to consumers.

An additional type of licensing is music. **Music Licensing** is a bit different from the earlier mentioned forms of licensing because it consists of three components. The first component is the original score, which is the lyrics, second is the performance of the music, and the third is the overall production. This is a complicated category that is well understood by those in that industry.

Moving along, the next type of licensing is **Celebrity Licensing**. Beyoncé, over the course of her career has certainly extended herself into the home through her fragrances, apparel, accessories and athletic wear. She is top-game, as it relates to celebrities, and has taken herself from a high position to an even higher position. So, when brand owners or licensees come to her, they know that she is well loved, respected, and able to demand a higher royalty rate and a higher performance level overall because of her competence and her fans.

Finally, the last type of licensing mentioned in this chapter is **Sports Licensing.** This type of licensing is comprised of major sports in the USA like baseball, basketball, football, and hockey. All of these sports are exciting to watch, but the world's greatest sport, football, also called soccer in the USA, captures the attention of huge brands. The FIFA World Cup played in Russia in 2018 and like the Olympics commanded a global audience. These sports brands want the opportunity to enable fans to consume them outside of their marquee event. In order to do this, the properties extend and expand, often through licensing.

So, these are all the types of brand licensing. As you think about your company, consider which category is most compatible with your brand.

*** 

So, what is Brand Licensing? Simply put, it is the relationship between you and the manufacturer. This legal relationship involves the brand lending itself to a third-party manufacturer in a particular category in exchange for royalty revenue payments. These payments are typically a percentage of net sales but can also be measured in a variety of different ways.

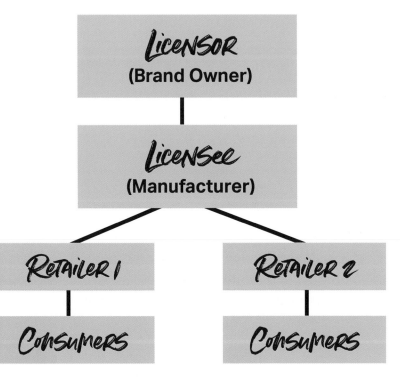

*Figure 1-2 Role Players*

Now that the types of brand licensing have been identified, let's discuss each **Role Player** in the process. We will use an example where the brand owner is Nike, and the manufacturer is the one who produces athletic apparel. As we know, Nike is a powerful brand that started in running shoes and has expanded into tremendous number of categories today. Let's say, for this example, Nike goes to a manufacturer who produces athletic apparel in an effort to expand their brand. In response, the manufacturer agrees to license Nike because they are familiar with Nike's reputations and know that this will benefit both parties. So, Nike along with the manufacturer consummate a binding relationship. Once the relationship has been established the licensee (manufacturer) then talks to retailers to create a program in their retail stores. Since Nike is well known by many, the retailer happily agrees and then arranges a relationship where they purchase the product and put it on their shelves. After the retailer agrees to host the brand in its store, the focus shifts to the consumer because consumers drive the consumption and success of all consumer brands. The consumers are the ones that make the final decision, have the personal relationship with the brands, buy the merchandise that is sold to the retailers by the manufacturer, and use their wallets to make the brands successful.

Now that we have discussed the Role Players and how their relationship works let's talk about how the **Licensed Product Flows.** Once the relationship is consummated, whether directly through you or an agency you choose, the licensee will start to develop concepts of what the product should look like. When these concepts are approved, prototypes will then be created for review and decisions will be made to reject or approve each prototype. Next, the final production run samples are tested to ensure that the product meets all quality and safety standards. In the final step, both you and the licensee agree on the finished product to ensure the product is safe to be sold and placed into the retail market. Thereby making the product available to be sold to the consumer. That's the flow of how the products are created.

| Licensor picks the product categories to be licensed | Licensor or its agent finds and negotiates a license with the best licensees | Licensees develop concepts, prototypes and final production samples and submit for approval | Licensor approves licensed products for sale | Licensees sell licensed product in authorized channels to retailers |

*Figure 1-3 - Licensed Product Flow*

**Royalty Payments Flow** is another important process included in brand licensing. To demonstrate this flow let's refer to the following example. In this particular example, the consumer buys Disney branded polo shirt at a retailer for $50. When the entire initial shipment of 200,000 polo shirts are sold the retailer's stores, that constitutes $10M worth of sold merchandise, which the retailer receives from consumers. Of that, the retailer paid $5M for that product from the manufacturer who licensed the brand from Walt Disney. The retailer marked it up a 100 percent to get their 50 percent margin. That $5M of merchandise that was bought by the retailer from the manufacturer generates $500,000 in royalties for Walt Disney based on a 10 percent royalty rate, which the manufacturer agreed to pay for the Disney brand.

Once the Purchase Order (PO) from the retailer is issued to the manufacturer, who licensed the brand, and the payment is made, the manufacturer will pay Walt Disney $500,000 in royalties for the merchandise that they sold. That's how the Payment Flow works. Hopefully, that is pretty straightforward and gives you a good idea of how this process works.

| The Tee Shirt and Cap Licensee pays Disney, the Licensor $500,000 in royalties ($5 million x 10% rate) | The Tee Shirt and Cap Licensee sells $5 million of licensed product to Sears and Target (based on 100% markup) | Retailers such as Sears and Target sell $10 million of licensed product e.g. Tee Shirts and Caps in a calendar year. |
|---|---|---|

*Figure 1-4 - Royalty Payment Flow*

In 2017, $271.6B in **Royalty Revenue** was generated globally.3 This is an increase of 3.3 percent from 2016. Of this, $157.7B in revenue was generated by North America (the US and Canada), meaning that North American leads with a total of 58 percent of Royalty Revenue. However, even though North American is leading the pack, the increase from 2016 to 2017 of 3.5 percent was relatively small compared to the other territories. The strongest increases from 2016 to 2017 were from North Asia (up 6.2 percent) and Latin America (up 7.6 percent).3 These statistics show that brand licensing in these two countries are on a strong trajectory. If they continue increasing at this pace, it could mean a major brand licensing shift. The different categories which are the largest include Entertainment/Character licensing, Corporate/Brands, and Fashion.

| Property | 2017 | | 2016 | | |
| | Retail Sales | Percentage of Total | Retail Sales | Percentage of Total | 2015 to 2016 Change |
| --- | --- | --- | --- | --- | --- |
| US / Canada | $157,662 | 58.0% | $152,284 | 57.9% | 3.5% |
| Western Europe | $53,233 | 19.6% | $52,363 | 19.9% | 1.7% |
| N Asia | 26,049 | 9.6% | $24,522 | 9.3% | 6.2% |
| LATAM | $10,716 | 3.9% | $9,958 | 3.8% | 7.6% |
| Eastern Europe | $9,531 | 3.5% | $9,802 | 3.7% | -2.8% |
| SEA/PAC | $9,349 | 3.4% | $8,970 | 3.4% | 4.2% |
| ME/Africa | $4,790 | 1.8% | $4,606 | 1.8% | 4.0% |
| ROW | $308 | 0.1% | $374 | 0.1% | -17.6% |
| Total WW | $271,638 | 100.0% | $262,880 | 100.0% | 3.3% |

Notes:
1) Ukraine, Kazakhstan and Romania removed from Argentina, Nigeria and Egypt added to 2017, regions adjusted as appropriate

*Revenue from Global Sales of Licensed Goods and Services, By Region, 2017. Source: LIMA*

\*\*\*

*Licensed Mickey Mouse Products; Source: Google Images*

Where did Brand Licensing get its origins?[5] Back in the late 1920's and 1930's when movies were first made, people began being exposed to consumer brands that were created. Think about old movies you watched as a child or even return to watching as an adult; what brands do you remember? Brands also originated from comic books and comic strips. These comics connected with consumers so intensely that consumers wanted to connect more with their favorite characters by buying a piece of licensed merchandise such as a tee-shirt or a cap. Then the television was invented and watching TV became yet another place that consumers connected with brands. Take a moment to think about the origins of the Walt Disney Company. What character comes to mind? Was your first thought about Mickey Mouse? Many are. Originally the Mickey Mouse character started to expand into licensed merchandise when people fell in love with the character. Just like the comic books and comic strips, consumers wanted more. The Walt Disney Company took full advantage of the opportunity and is now a dominant consumer product goods, much if not all of their products sold are officially licensed merchandise. They have a tremendous number of characters and continue to be innovative in the marketplace.

What happened after? Well, corporations saw that consumers wanted merchandise integrated with the specific characters they adored. So, corporations asked themselves, "How do we conduct commerce? How do we benefit from this industry? And, how do we fulfill the demand in the marketplace that the consumers are wanting?" To start, companies contacted the brand owners and created relationships that enabled merchandise to be created in the marketplace that consumers wanted to buy.

As time, technology, and trends changed, brand licensing grew. Below are a few examples using food and automotive licensing. Take a glance at Breyers frozen yogurt. Traditionally Breyers has been known as an ice cream brand. However, a third- party manufacturer who makes yogurt suggested that they make frozen yogurt with the Breyers name. This proved to be a very beneficial relationship for Breyers because consumers want to eat a little bit healthier. Frozen yogurt is considered to be a healthier alternative to ice cream and now, with this partnership, Breyers consumers who live a healthier lifestyle can purchase frozen yogurt from a brand that they love and trust. Similarly, in the second example, TGI Fridays, which has a very successful restaurant chain has been given permission by consumers to expand into frozen goods sold at retailers to enable consumers to gain more access to the brand. Now if consumers are craving appetizers, entrees, or desserts from TGI Fridays, the option to purchase these items at their local grocer is available. The last example is with Eddie Bauer and Ford. Eddie Bauer is known for being rugged and Ford is known as a quality and reliable automobile manufacturer. Together both brands benefit by Eddie Bauer and Ford entering into a

*Breyers and T.G.I. Fridays Licensed Products;*
*8 Source: Google Images*

licensing relationship.

✳✳✳

What drives the success of brands? As a brand owner, it's critical that you understand your **Brand Positioning.** If the Brand Position is right everything else will follow in a successful fashion. If you are unable to determine the Brand Position then the communication between the brand and consumer will not be understandable, ultimately affecting the consumer's perception of the brand. If this happens, consumers will decide the Brand Position instead of the brand. This unintended consequence creates an enormous amount of confusion in the marketplace. So, defining the Brand Positioning sets the foundation for everything else that follows, making the Brand Positioning critical to the success of brand licensing as well.

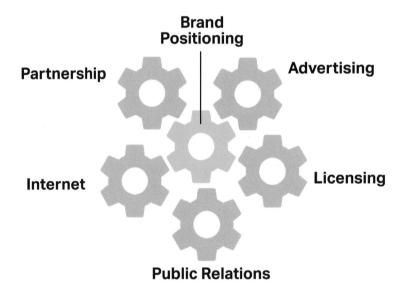

*Figure 1-5 Brand Positioning Drives Success*

Mr. Clean is a Proctor and Gamble (P&G) owned brand that has been around since 1957. P&G decided that the Mr. Clean Brand Positioning would focus on helping families to clean the toughest dirt spots. If mom or dad needs to clean their floors, they know Mr. Clean can help them get it done the way it needs to be, without any concerns about sanitation or damage to their floor–

ing. Consumers feel this way because Mr. Clean has become a trusted and adored brand. As a result, the Mr. Clean brand manager and the P&G brand team deliberated on categories that would help to expand the brand while reinforcing the brand's position. The list of categories (shown below) that Mr. Clean has been able to extend into provided a better solution for the consumer. Mr. Clean has done so well that it has extended the brand into categories like mops, rubber gloves, buckets, and now automotive car washes. This is a fantastic example of brand licensing done well.

*Mr. Clean Licensed Products: Source: Google Images*

Now, how about an example that's not such a good example? The Stanley brand in this particular example does not look like it was executed at the same level as the Mr. Clean brand. What happened here is that Stanley said: "Look we have a strong brand in the marketplace. We want to benefit from brand licensing. We have had some disappointing sales results. How can we strengthen our overall financial position?" To accomplish these tasks, Stanley decided to bring in a licensing agency. However, the agency did not completely understand or focus on Stanley's Brand Positioning. Stanley, instead, entered a variety of categories including portable fans, desk organizers, and Christmas lights timers. Ultimately these created a misunderstanding of what Stanley stood for and represented. The results were devastating, mainly

*Stanley Poorly Licensed Products;*
*Source: Google Images*

because none of these categories coincided with the Brand Positioning. Because the Brand Positioning was not identified at the point of licensing, the brand extensions were in unrelated categories causing a significant disconnect between the brand and the consumer, confusing consumers about what Stanley stands for in the marketplace and further harming the brand. Later, the Stanley brand focused on terrific hand tools and small tools aligned with their Brand Positioning and found success in the marketplace.

*Kendall Jenner Sporting adidas Fashion; Source HYPERBEAST*

Kendall Jenner signed a deal with Adidas as an Adidas Original Ambassador. Since she represents a brand herself, it is ideal for her to use licensing in order to grow her brand. In this case, Kendall is a non-athlete, but she is partnered with an athletic brand. One might think this is a bad move on Adidas part, but actually it makes perfect sense. Although Kendall is not an athlete she is fit, young, vibrant and represents a target of the market that Adidas is unable to reach. Many people today who wear Adidas do not consider themselves athletes. So, signing with Jenner encourages non-athletic consumers to purchase the Adidas brand for daily wear, fashion, and athletic purposes. If I had to guess, I would say that Adidas is trying to reposition their brand one step at a time. We don't know enough information to be certain, but think about the challenges the brand could face as it relates to its brand position. Questions that might be relevant to answer concerning this case are, "How successful will the Adidas brand be with Kendall Jenner?" and, "How does this partnership reinforce Kendall's Brand Positioning in the marketplace?"

***

Why Brand Licensing? Why should you license into new categories? There are a variety of reasons for you to license your brand. If your brand has a high preference, licensing enables you to unlock your brands' latent value and satisfy pent-up demand. Through licensing, you have the ability to enter new categories practically overnight, gaining an immediate brand presence on store shelves and often in the media. Brand licensing also enables you to try out potential new businesses or geographical markets with relatively small up-front risk. By licensing your brand to a third-party manufacturer, you can try new businesses, or move into new countries with a smaller up-front investment than by building and staffing its own operations. You might want to know why manufacturers would choose to license? For manufacturers, the list of benefits is equally extensive. Licensing offers immediate credibility and recognition, enabling licensees to enter new markets while enhancing sales of their core products. Consider a tee-shirt manufacturer with specialty printing capabilities. One day they are selling unbranded tee-shirts; the next they are an official Disney licensee creating shirts with Mickey Mouse and Winnie the Pooh. Licensees also gain authenticity and legitimacy through well-known brands that consumers trust.

Here, is an example of brand expansion using the M&M'S brand. M&M'S is one of the greatest brands in the marketplace. Their advertising is best in class; they portray feelings of fun and happiness, and when consumed, they provide good experiences to the consumer. The M&M'S brand is great alone, but if the brand didn't create programs for growth, the brand could possibly enter a state of under-optimization. To avoid this and increase growth M&M'S licensed their brand to a third-party manufacturer to produce the iconic little characters and jackets. In another example, M&M'S has taken other brands and brought them on. For instance, M&M'S chose to license with a variety of brands to put on their candy product. This now allows consumers to go to their website, make an account, and customize M&M'S with the brand that they love. So, if a fan of the Philadelphia Eagles wanted M&M'S with that brand, they could do that. Now M&M'S is able to connect with a wide array of

*m&m's Licensed Products: Source: Google Images*

consumers in the way consumers want, both literally and figuratively.

For M&M'S, these types of licensing arrangements propelled their brand out in the marketplace in the categories they wouldn't be in otherwise. This makes the brand more consumable and enjoyable by their consumers. Each licensing program benefits the licensor by allowing the brand to connect with fans in more ways, which not only builds brand equity but also drives royalty revenue.

Another potential benefit to you, the licensor, could include access to knowledge and insights held by the licensee. They may know a manufacturing or marketing technique that can be incorporated into your own go to market strategy. You now have an inside view of what happens throughout their organization and how they perform their tasks. Also, you have a preview of any newly created technology or innovative products that the licensee intends to develop with your brand. Lastly, you are granted direct access to the strong relationships that the licensee has built over time, which affords you the opportunity to create relationships in channels that were unobtainable previously. Having insight into this knowledge can prove to be profitable to your ongoing business.

This concludes the first phase chapter of *Breakthrough Licensing*. We hope that you found it interesting. If you are ready, let's move onto the next chapter, The 8-Step Brand Licensing Process.

# Chapter 2
# The 8-Step Brand Licensing Process

Brand licensing can be beneficial for both licensors (brand owners) and licensees (companies which sell official licensed products) if done in a step-by-step manner. In this chapter of **Breakthrough Licensing**, I will provide you with a detailed overview of the 8-Step Brand Licensing Process so you can begin to see how to achieve your brand licensing goals. Each section is brief, yet comprehensive, and clarifies where attention should be focused while also displaying examples that will increase your knowledge and understanding. Let's begin.

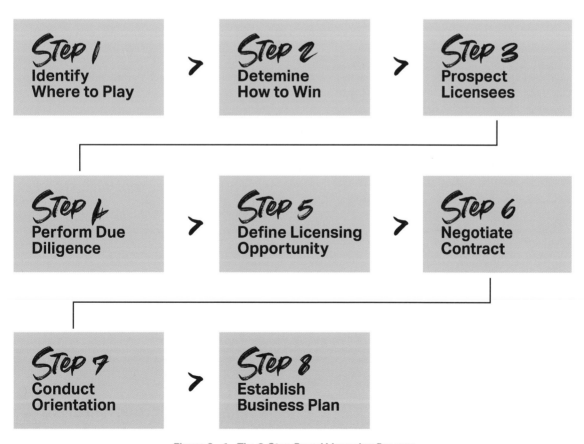

*Figure 2 - 1 - The 8-Step Brand Licensing Process*

# Step 1: Identify Where to Play

When consumers become delighted by a particular brand's experience, they begin to bond emotionally with the brand. They become brand loyalists and advocates, buying the brand more often and recommending it to others. This behavior serves to build the brand's reputation. The stronger the reputation, the higher the value of the brand and the greater revenue it will drive for its owner. One important fundamental fact to remember about licensing is that only the strongest brands are candidates to be licensed. So, if your brand is not strong, well-known, or loved by consumers, it might be better to stop, take a step back and look for alternate ways to tell your brand's story so that it can expand, extend, and grow. If your path leads to these alternative paths, don't get discouraged. Storytelling allows your brand to gain awareness and name recognition. The key is to follow effective marketing strategies and tactics such as creative advertising campaigns to reach the target market. If however, your brand is strong, it will be permitted to extend and expand into categories that complement its original offering.

*NFL and Verizon partnership; Source: Google Images*

Verizon is doing a terrific job of aligning the brand with its position. Regardless of the category that Verizon is in, they stand for something. The brand is fresh, relevant, trending, and uniquely connects with their consumers. These characteristics are exceptional since consumers will search out and buy Verizon in a host of different categories due to the connection they have developed with the brand. Understanding where to play, and what extension opportunities are afforded, allows the brand to grow.

# Step 2: Determine How to Win

Once the product category, the one that satisfies the brand extension goals and creates positive associations for your brand has been identified, the next step is to determine how to go about executing the extension. Before entering the product development process, you must evaluate whether your company has enough resources to complete the endeavor. If a substantial amount of resources is not available, it may be better to choose an alternative route. There is nothing worse than terminating the project midway due to lack of resources. If your company does not possess the capability to produce the product internally, external options are available.

There are two primary ways to extend the brand externally. The first is to acquire a company that is currently commercializing the product. The advantages of this option include having the manufacturing, marketing, and selling of the product under one roof, which means quality control and costs can be more easily managed. One of the disadvantages of acquiring a company is that you need to have a sufficient amount of cash to complete the transaction. Additionally, this external option can require a significant amount of time to consummate, and even if the transaction is completed there still could be inadequate resources allocated for marketing the product, thereby restricting your ability to move forward. Finally, the integration of an acquired company can often be tedious and difficult to accomplish. The second option you could choose is to license the brand to a manufacturer of the product in the same category. The advantages of this option are the investment risks are lower and the manufacturer, or licensee, possesses the capability to manufacture not only the product but also market it. The license also possesses the necessary relationships with distributors and retailers to make a success of the program. The disadvantage of this option is you must relinquish some control to the licensee and you will give up profit margin. As a brand owner, it is your responsibility to determine which option best fits your licensing needs.

# Step 3: Prospect Licenses

Once a product category has been identified, and brand licensing is the preferred method to achieve this extension, it is time to scout for prospective licensees. In this step it is necessary to develop a basic checklist. Among other things you should evaluate the prospective licensee against the following parameters:

- Stragetic Reasoning
- Size and financial strength
- Market share in the product category
- Current or previous licenses held
- Awards received
- Consumer perception

Once your checklist has been created, identifying companies that manufacture in the selected product category will be the next step. In this stage you will research manufacturers that are positioned in the area you have chosen. For a manufacturer, understanding the consumers' wants and devising a solution to meet these wants plays a significant role in whether or not you should add them to your consideration list of prospective licensees. The best places to identify these prospects include researching the Internet, Trade Directories, Trade Magazines, Trade Shows, and Research Companies. You may also conduct a market tour to physically see what products are on retailers' shelves. As a licensor, you should observe and evaluate the licensees' products to determine if they are well placed in the right channels.

# Step 4: Conduct Due Diligence

Once manufacturers are identified and located, the Due Diligence process can begin to determine which licensees will progress to the next phase. The Due Diligence stage involves evaluation of prospective licensees' businesses from a financial, legal, and risk management perspective. The more comprehensive the evaluation, the less likely the licensee selected will have unforeseen issues going forward. Each licensee should be required to complete a rigorous Licensing Application that requests detailed information on all aspects of the prospective licensee's company. This application should involve:

- An assessment of the company's o Strategic reasoning
  - Financial strength
  - Marketing acumen
  - Operational capability
- A high-level forecast of licensed product sales. If the size is not sufficient to justify the investment, then additional efforts to secure this company as a licensee may be in vain.

After this rigorous application is completed and signed, the licensee must stand behind the statements given to you. As I imagine, you have spent millions if not billions of dollars on building your brand over years, and in some instances, decades. It is your primary goal to make sure that your partner will enhance your brand and not hurt it. This is why you should ensure you have a rigorous application for a prospective licensee to complete and sign. The application also serves to separate the curious from the serious eliminating wasted time.

# Step 5: Define Licensing Opportunity

After the Due diligence phase is completed, you should ideally be left with two or three qualified prospects. Determining which candidate best adheres to the brand's needs is not an easy task. This is often the case when all the candidates look strong. To further assist in deciding which candidate is best suited, you must assess the size and scope of the actual licensed product program by working closely with the candidate licensees to understand their strengths and weaknesses.

Outstanding candidates will immerse themselves in your brand gaining a full understanding of the Brand Positioning, Promise and Architecture. The licensing program presented to the licensor should include the proposed look and feel of the licensed products, and incorporate the brand's attributes into the design of their products. When defining the opportunity see if the licensees pay particular attention to the details, such as the placement of the logo on the product, how it is affixed, and the material from where it is constructed. Remember that the smallest of details separates the average licensee from the outstanding licensee. Additionally, an astute licensee will request that you provide them with the brand's style guide so they have the required information to create concepts that will represent the brand accurately.

## Step 6: Negotiate Deal Terms & Finalize Contract

Now that the Licensing Opportunity is established, it is time to determine the core deal terms. These parameters define the structure of the contract, including:

- The term of the contract
- Where the licensed products will be sold
- What royalty rate will be paid
- What trademarks will be used

Because these terms are unique to every licensing contract, they must be negotiated between you and the prospective licensee for each contract.

While each party inherently wants to arrive at the most favorable terms for their side, the best set of Deal Terms are those that allow both parties to achieve a successful long-term licensing program. As a successful licensor, you want to keep the end in mind and practice win- win negotiating strategies. If the other party feels like you are benefiting more from the partnership than they are, chances are that the deal will not succeed long-term or will not proceed. Smart licensees will have identified several choices of brands from which they plan to acquire a license and will set limits on what deal terms they will accept, regardless of the brand.

Assuming that both parties agree on the terms of the contract, the deal terms are acknowledged in writing and then passed to an attorney to place into your licensing contract template. This template should include all other terms and conditions such as Confidential Information, Representations and Warranties, etc.

# Step 7: Orientation

The execution of the contract signifies the beginning of the relationship. It is therefore vital for the licensee to get as familiar as possible with your brand and the licensing program. It is equally important for you to provide the licensee with the information needed to be successful. Orientation provides opportunities for key members of your company and the licensee's company to meet, get to know one another, and review expectations and contractual requirements. During the orientation session, you and the licensee should listen actively, ask questions, and get answers. In this session, the licensee typically provides an overview of the staff and resources dedicated to the program, the Product Forecast, the Marketing Plan, and the Product Concepts. Alternatively, you will typically provide the Brand Architecture, the Brand Positioning, the Category Positioning, the Timelines, the Key Terms, the Review of Testing and Auditing Protocol, the Approval Process, and the Licensing Style Guide.

A strong and enduring relationship is never built in a day. It is an ongoing process that takes time. However, the more you and licensee interact with each other during the orientation and ongoing, the more successful the relationship and licensing program will be.

# Step 8: Business Planning

The Business Planning phase defines what gets measured. Monitoring the licensee's business and ensuring that they set achievable targets serves to empower the licensee to maximize the license successfully. They will grow to appreciate this over time.

To begin, the licensee should start by developing a one-year business plan that is founded on your Brand and Category Positioning Statements. The Minimum Sales, Minimum Guarantees, and Royalty Rate should also be included in this plan to make an accurate forecast and to set realistic goals. Projected Royalties should also be calculated based on the Sales Projections and reviewed against Minimum Royalties to assess the robustness of the plan. The Business Plan must be appropriately structured to allow you and the licensee to work together in a seamless partnership that enables the plan to be successful.

When I ran the Rubbermaid global licensing business, I would hold a monthly review with each licensee, which they had to prepare reports. During this routine call, we would discuss our progress, our challenges and our successes for the month and for the year. A comparison between their actual sales results versus what they said we were going to accomplish illuminated why we overachieved or why we didn't meet expectations. We constantly assessed why our expectations were not met and therefore what we could do to course correct so that the overall success for the full year was achieved. Our quarterly reviews were more rigorous. The licensee would be expected to review the prior quarter across a number of criteria. This assessment allowed us to adapt and evolve so that we would be successful.

Now that we have reviewed the 8-Step Brand Licensing Process we will review the Brand Licensing Timeline. A large portion of the Brand Licensing Timeline involves the 8-Step Brand Licensing Process (first 14 months). The first three months of this timeline is fixated on *Identifying Where to Play*. These first three months are crucial to the foundation of your licensing program, so be sure to take your time as you locate and or define the Brand Essence – the heart and soul of the brand – , Brand Positioning, Brand Extension, and Brand Identity. These allotted three months provide you with an adequate amount of time to set the groundwork. Determining *How to Win*, is the next phase of the Timeline and takes about a month to complete. This step in the process provides you with tools to help you decide how you want to play the game. In other words, what method works best for you; is it *acquiring* or *licensing*? The decision that you make will decide if you move to other steps in this 8-Step Brand Licensing Process of maneuver another route as you *acquire*. Another month is allocated to *Prospect Licensing* to find prospective licensees which you hope will provide the answers to your needs and a fit to your organization. The next two months is all about *Performing Due Diligence*. Now that you have gathered a pool of qualified licensees, or so you think, this stage reveals the good, bad, and ugly of the licensees' organizations and if they are curious or serious about licensing. *Defining Licensing Opportunity* takes another two-months and uses both the Licensee Application and The Conservative Business Estimator to learn the size of the opportunity each prospective licensee expects. As you continue the process, the next month is dedicated to *Negotiating Deal Terms*. Negotiations are different for every partnership, but creating a "win-win" situation in this portion of the Timeline is key. After this stage, two more months are set aside to *Agree Deal Terms*; the language is very important.

Once completed the contract can be signed and you are off to the next step in the process, *Conducting Orientation*, which falls into the second twelve-month period. Orientation provides a clear understanding of the expectations that both you and the licensee have moving forward. Once you have completed the Orientation, *Concept Development* starts; the prototypes are developed; they are Approved; samples are sent, and those samples are then shared with retailers, typically during a *Line Review*. Retailers then select which samples they want to purchase and the program starts coming to life. When the retailer issues a *Purchase Order* to the manufacturer (also known as the licensee), they will know the quantity to produce and ship. Once *Approved*, the *Production* and *Shipping* take place and leads to the Commercialization phase; this phase involves the Approval process as outlined in the contract. This Brand Licensing Timeline can be shorter than the 24-month period shown below, but is can also be longer. So, it's like anything else, ramp-up time has to be built in on the front end, but once that's established and ongoing, your business with the licensee (the manufacturer) is going to grow, evolve, and be successful. Some of these relationships can even continue for decades.

*Figure 2 -2 - The Brand Licensing Timeline*

By this point you should now have a good understanding of the process and what is needed to be successful. I look forward to taking you through the next chapter of this program.

# Chapter 3
# Ten Pitfalls of Brand Licensing

Ever witness a brand's business, reputation, or licensing program being damaged, but were uncertain of the reasons why? Most likely it could have been caused by one or more brand licensing pitfalls. In this chapter of **Breakthrough Licensing**, I will take you, the brand owner through the ten most frequently experienced **Brand Licensing Pitfalls** that should be avoided when operating under a licensing agreement. It is my hope that once these are read and understood, you will have an adequate amount of knowledge on the subject to discern if you are engaging in, or teetering near, a pitfall.

***

## Pitfall 1: Biting Off More Than You Can Chew

This scenario happens when a manufacturer desires a license from you so badly that they are willing to commit to anything they think you want to see in their application and projections in order to acquire that license. When this happens, you are likely going to be enamored with the manufacturer's projections and will want to leap at the opportunity to incorporate this potentially huge and successful licensing program with your brand. However, what you may not know is that the manufacturer isn't in any way capable of actually achieving those results. By not being able to count on the projections, you inadvertently place the brand in a volatile situation when the projections offered by manufacturer are not delivered. So, what's likely to happen? The manufacturer is not going to achieve the results; they are not going to meet their Guaranteed Minimums Sales or Royalty Commitments, and the program is going to collapse on itself.

This disingenuous submission harms the manufacturer's reputation by placing them in the category of overpromising and under delivering, but it also leaves you under-compensated for the work and resources you have invested into this license. When a licensee is unable to succeed, they may terminate the license, and while you can sue to extract the Minimum Guaranteed Royalties in a settlement down the line; this is not what you expect or want to occur. You want a successful licensee who will put the branded merchandise in the marketplace where consumers are able to purchase and fall in love with the brand, which leads to purchases of other branded products. Even though the licensee might have bit off more than they could chew, you lose just as much, if not more. To avoid this pitfall the manufacturer should be realistic about their projections. It is always better for all parties involved to be honest about the size and scale of the licensing program even if it costs the license.

## Pitfall 2: Getting In Over Your Head

While this may seem the same as "Pitfall 1", it isn't. In this case, the manufacturer informs you of the channels they desire to secure in the agreement. Instead of limiting their selection to the channel or channels that provide the most financial success and benefit, the manufacturer over-extends into channels that make sense to you, but which they're unable to commercialize. This leaves these channels (or territories or categories) barren of licensed product, precluding consumers from engaging with the brand. Therefore, it is best for the licensee to start out in a channel (or territories or categories) that offers the highest chance for growth and success for the brand and then ask you for more channels, categories or deal terms once the parameters in the agreement are achieved. This demonstrated success means the likelihood of getting the additional channels (or territories or categories) will be high.

## Pitfall 3: Having Unrealistic Expectations

Unrealistic expectations happen when the licensee doesn't understand the strength of the brand they have acquired the rights to. The licensee may think they have a great new product and know that with the help of your brand they will be successful. Without an ample understanding of the strength of the brand, or its success, position, and growth, the license could set goals for itself that are unachievable.

Licensees are not the only ones that can set unrealistic expectations; you can also. Let's face it, the competition in the marketplace is continually increasing, and with the help of technology and the Internet, any well-managed brand can gain a share of the market if they have the resources. This phenomenon has caused many brand owners to feel like they have no other choice but to set goals that are out of reach and force themselves to try and exceed them. Unfortunately, this only diminishes the brand and leaves them feeling unaccomplished.

Another unrealistic expectation that you can have is assuming that any best-in-class licensee you have chosen as a candidate will want to license your brand. This licensee may be strong in the market, capable of successfully carrying out the licensing program, positioned in all the right channels, and even directly expressed interest in your brand. However, certain factors such as a change in organizational leadership, the acquisition of your competitor, or unexpected financial missteps could prohibit a licensing agreement.

Having the right realistic expectation propels the brand forward creating the desired outcome. Don't think that the brand will get everything done just because it is highly regarded with a successful track record. It takes work, realistic goals, and much more.

## Pitfall 4: Logo Slapping

Now most of us have been exposed to the term "logo slapping." Logo slapping occurs when a licensee acquires a brand and affixes the brand's logo onto any newly developed product and does not take the time to build the brand's attributes into the product. Some licensees believe that putting a famous logo on any product will produce high sales and profits, for them, and corresponding royalties for you. However, this is not at all true. Consumers are intelligent and can decipher when a newly developed product doesn't work with the brand. When consumers ultimately do not buy these newly licensed products, the equity in the brand erodes, which costs both parties resources and profit. Instead of logo slapping, licensees should custom design the brand's attributes into the product. Secondly, they should treat the licensed brand as if it were their own. Thirdly, they should follow the brand's style guide carefully. And finally, the licensee should develop a licensed product that everyone would be proud to sell or consume. The licensee should provide you with a physical and digital prototype of the product before a massive production takes place. This measure will ensure that they have created an innovative product that includes the attributes of the brand and follows the style guide.

As the licensor, it is imperative that you decipher the licensee's intentions with your brand before entering into a contract. If, they want to acquire a license for the purposes of using your logo to sell products that do not incorporate your brand's attributes or reference your Brand Positioning, avoid them at all cost. This precautionary step will help you dodge this pitfall.

## Pitfall 5: Failure To Follow The Approval Process

The Approval Process you set forth is in place for many reasons. Licensees failing to understand and follow the approval process fully according to the specifications given could result in the products not being approved. This can be frustrating to the licensee and cause them to sell the unapproved products. Selling unapproved products can be very costly. For instance, consumers could file lawsuits against you and licensee, if they cause harm or fail to meet a government standard.

Many times this can occur due to a licensee's lack of knowledge rather than an intentional act. Let's be honest, the licensing contract is a boring document to read. However, it is necessary that the licensee is aware of the Approval Process. This is the reason why Step 7, **Conducting Orientation**, in the 8-Step Brand Licensing Process is a must. Orientation will give you the opportunity to explain to the licensee and their team the reasons why an Approval Process is needed, the steps in the Approval Process, and stress that an Approval Process must take place before a product is created and placed in the market. Even though a licensee might commit this act unintentionally, in no way should you condone or absolve this behavior.

While there may be moments where the Approval Process is overlooked unintentionally, there are times when a licensee can be deceitful and avoid the Approval Process to meet their sales goals. Staying involved in the creation process and communicate with the licensee on a constant basis to help reduce this pitfall. This level of engagement will also help them to avoid improper planning that can result in missing modular shipping and sales dates.

## PITFALL 6: NOT KNOWING THE CONTRACT

Many different components are included in a contract such as terms, the Approval Process, the location in which the product will be sold, the Royalty Rate to be paid, the trademark to be used, and much more. Being unfamiliar with the contract can unknowingly strain the licensing relationship and ultimately result in termination of the contract. To avoid this pitfall ensure you and the licensee are familiar with the terms and obligations in the contract. This includes members of the sales, marketing, product development, and design teams.

## PITFALL 7: NOT PREPARED TO INVEST INTO THE LICENSE

Let's say you and the licensee reach a point where the license is acquired, the Orientation is completed, and the Business Plan is finalized. By this point both parties have invested a substantial amount of time (6 - 18 months)

preparing for a successful license. At this point there are high expectations by both parties. If either one or both parties have not allocated enough resources for the budget there is a high likelihood the program will fail. Any licensee you choose must plan to invest just as much as you in the newly acquired brand in proportion to the agreement. You expect the licensee to drive sales and brand growth while pursuing every channel and every category designated by the contract. In turn, the licensee expects you to market the brand, to provide support during sales calls and quick approvals. Avoiding this pitfall is simple if you both establish accountability within your organizations and match each party's level
of investment.

## Pitfall 8: Selling In Unauthorized Channels

Licensees who are unaware of the terms of the contract usually make the mistake of selling in unauthorized channels. Often times what happens is the licensee encounters another licensee who is also selling in the same channel, resulting in a significant amount of confusion in the marketplace. One way to avoid this pitfall is to have full knowledge of the contracts terms, conditions, and boundaries. Second, prevent the sale of licensed products outside the authorized channels or territories by incorporating stiff penalties in your licensing contracts, up to and including termination.

## Pitfall 9: Trusting That The Licensor Has Your Best Interest At Heart

Let's remember that everyone is in this business of meeting their own business objectives and to drive shareholder value. Sometimes licensees have their own agenda that may not be aligned with your agenda. Be aware! A licensee may have ulterior motives such as using you to gain access to your customers and developed relationships because they have strained their relationships. Don't assume that just because the contract was signed, you and the licensee are entirely aligned. Be thorough and ask the right questions to ensure you both share the same vision and values.

# Pitfall 10: Not Following The Written Contract

Everything you and the manufacturer agreed upon is drawn up into a written contract, which explicitly states the regulations of the licensing program. Sometimes licensees decide to cut corners for one reason or another even though they know what the written contract states.

Example: The brand owner calls the licensee up and says, "I want you to ship products to Argentina." The licensee knows that the rights to ship products to Argentina are not in their contract, but they choose to do it anyhow because they received a verbal request from the brand owner. Weeks later the licensee is called in for a meeting with a person in the brand owner's organization to be told, "The shipment that was sent to Argentina was not in your contract. You are going to be penalized for all the sales you made in that country." Even though the licensee explained that the shipment was at the brand owner's request, it was not in the contract or in written form.

Not following the written contract can put the licensee in a bad situation or have a devastating financial impact to the licensee depending on the loss of revenue or the amount of the penalties they are required to pay. Anytime you make a verbal request to the licensee, you should always put it in writing to ensure they have the right. They can also achieve this by asking you to send an email confirming the request. So, word to the wise, follow the written contract!

Those are the ten pitfalls of brand licensing. If you can avoid these pitfalls you are going to be in a great position to be successful.

# Chapter 4
# Identify Where to Play

In the 8-Step Brand Licensing Process, identifying "Where to Play" is the first step towards establishing any successful brand licensing program. This step helps you, the brand owner, set a strong foundation as you begin to create a brand licensing program that will enable growth in untapped markets. On the surface it may seem as if this step is elementary, but do not disregard it. Just like a house needs a solid foundation to stand, so does a brand licensing program. Moving forward, the Essence of The Brand, Brand Positioning, Brand Extension, and Brand Identity will be explained.

When identifying "Where to Play", the first question you should ask is, "What is the **Essence Of The Brand**?" In simpler terms what does this brand mean to you, to others in your organization, to your customers, and to its consumers? Do consumers and customers find the brand differentiated and relevant compared to the competition? Take Coca-Cola, Google, and Apple for instance. Each brand's essence is different from the other and means different things to the people in whom they are in contact. Coca-Cola's Brand Essence is centered on creating happiness and acceptance, Google's Brand Essence is to empower people by making the world's information universally accessible, and Apple's essence emanates from their tagline to *Think Different*, and while the Essence of The Brands might seem simple they evoke feelings that translate to each brand's meaning. Obtaining a clear understanding of the Brand Essence is critical considering this starts the process of being able to create products consumers are going to want to purchase and that customers will put on their shelves.

**Brand Positioning** is an essential part of licensing a brand, and is defined as the arranging for a branded product to occupy a clear, distinctive, and desirable place relative to competing brands or products in the mind of a target consumer.2 If the brand's position is not clear, distinctive, or desirable it will not be successful, so it's imperative to develop the brand positioning correctly. A great example of brand positioning is P&G who owns six different brands of laundry detergent, which includes Tide, Cheer, Gain, Era, Dreft, and Ivory. Most people are surprised when they see these strong brands under the umbrella of P&G, but why have six brands of laundry detergent? Basically, because that's how many are needed in the marketplace to meet all of their consumer's need. This proves

*Types of P&G laundry detergent; Source: P&G website.*

that brands can all live in the same space, have different Brand Positioning and be successful. Each of these brands compete with each other, compete with other competitors' products, and features a different set and prioritization of benefits positioned at different segments. Let's take a glance at each brand individually.

- **Tide**: Fabric cleaning and care at its best.
- **Cheer**: Protection against fading, color transfer and fabric wear in powder or liquid, with or without bleach.
- **Gain**: Excellent cleaning power and a smell that says clean.
- **Era**: Powerful laundry detergent that is tough on stains.
- **Dreft**: Specially formulated detergent that rinses out thoroughly leaving clothes soft next to a baby's skin.
- **Ivory**: Mild cleansing benefits for a gentile, pure and simple clean.

Now take a moment and reflect over your own brand as you answer these questions. First, does your current branded product occupy a clear, distinctive, and desirable place relative to competing branded or unbranded products, in the mind of a target consumer? If yes, are you sure? If not, why not? Be honest with yourself in answering these questions. The more accurate they are, the better your program will be. An accurate Brand Positioning is critical to any program and foundationally indispensable to a brand licensing program's success as well. If the Brand Positioning is muddled or unclear trouble will follow; you will immediately see the lack of momentum and a degradation in the brand's performance.

There are three steps you can follow to build a solid Brand Positioning Statement. The first is to (1) *Identify The Target Market* by defining the category in which they are competing, which are the consumer segments, and what the target markets are. Once these are defined, then (2) *Define The Nature of The Competition* must be understood. While scoping out the competition make sure to focus on what type of products are out there and what the competition is doing in the marketplace. Also think about how your brand is different from the competition and why consumers would want to choose your branded product. Points of differentiation take brands that are similar and enable them reach a different audience. Every brand manager that desires to compete successfully has to determine at least four or five distinctions of the brand versus its competition. The last step is to (3) *Select A Positioning Strategy* to determine the combination of benefits that will give consumers the greatest value. This strategy should also consist of a developed Brand Positioning document and statement, along with a definition of the desired brand equity. Once the position is understood, entering marketplace will be relatively straightforward.

*Coca-Cola Brand Extensions; Source: TheJournal.ie*

After the Brand Essence and Brand Positioning are clarified, the next stage is to look at **Brand Extensions** that comply with the Brand Expansion Point, Brand Essence, and Brand Positioning. Currently two types of Brand Extensions exist that will help the brand optimize growth and profits. The first Brand Extension is a "Line" Extension. Coca-Cola, a favorite beverage of many, is a great illustration of a Line Extension. Coca-Cola's Line Extensions include Diet Coke, Cherry Coke, Coke Zero, and a very unusual one called Clear Coke for the consumers in Japan. All of the Line Extensions listed are extensions of a single primary product, which comes from the Coca-Cola brand. The extensions are variations of the core brand based on different formulations. They are then given a distinct position in the marketplace.

The second extension is "Category" Extension also known as brand expansion. Category Extensions are typically seen in brand licensing because brand owners like you are contemplating different categories that are not core to the business. Therefore, third-party manufacturers assist in your endeavor to get the brand into a particular category successfully. Crayola, for example, was known as the premier brand of crayons for decades and most of us grew up using Crayola crayons. Though the brand had been successful for decades, the opportunities afforded to it in the marketplace were substantial, meaning the brand was under-optimized. The Crayola team came up with a brilliant idea to extend into different categories through licensing. They knew from the start they could not manufacture the products themselves in the categories they were

*Crayola Category Extensions Products; Source: Crayola Website.*

entering (without a substantial investment) so, Crayola decided to find best-in-class licensing partners and let them extend the Crayola brand into those categories on their behalf. Due to this partnership Crayola has extended into variety of different categories using licensing. As a brand owner, it is important not to choose extensions that do not make sense to the brand. Said another way, be sure the extensions you choose follow the brand's expansion point and reinforce the brand's position, promise and essence.

*Mr. Clean Licensed Products; Source: Google Images*

Let's look at an example using Mr. Clean. Many people love Mr. Clean and for this reason it is a great brand to show how brand licensing works. The Mr. Clean promise is to get out the toughest stains making cleaning easier through well-designed products.

They do this by reinforcing the Brand Positioning through each of the different products they've extended into including mops, buckets, brooms, and other complementary products. Each of the Category Extensions reinforces the position of the brand making the products desirable in the marketplace. Not only do the extensions reinforce the position, but they also strengthen the core product, which is the Mr. Clean liquid cleaner. Additionally, through these extensions, Mr. Clean could gain new distribution channels because their brand licensing partners have competency and relationships in channels where Mr. Clean may not be currently sold. These existing distribution channels held by the Mr. Clean licensees make it easier for them to bring the Mr. Clean core product into these channels. Due to these created partnerships and manufacturer relationships Mr. Clean is able to expand its awareness through these newly launched products. As the Mr. Clean Brand Positioning is reinforced through the use of associative brand imagery the Mr. Clean Brand Equity is elevated. This creates a virtuous cycle resulting in new distribution through thousands of retail outlets.

Brand Extensions are beneficial in terms of growth, but much more is required in driving Brand Extension success. You must ask yourself, "Does the parent brand have positive associations in the consumers' memory?" Understanding whether the brand association within the new category is positive or negative provides information that determines whether the brand has an opportunity for extension. If positive associations are linked to a brand the likelihood of success in a new category is high. The positive association that support the brand in the new category will now drive its own association that will be remembered by consumers. Even though the positive associations are remembered, you should consider research to discover which positive associations are more favorable for the extensions. Understanding which associations are more favorable reveals whether the associations are unique enough that the brand brings a competitive advantage to the category. If it does then there is a chance of success in the new category.

As the brand owner, you should also evaluate the parent brand (associated with the core product) to see if the brand has any negative associations that will play a significant role in the consumers' evaluation of the new category. Negative associations that the core brand has might adversely impact the success of the Brand Extension. Another factor to consider is whether the new category results in negative associations that will erode the parent brand's equity. The Parent Brand Equity may be strong enough to allow for the extension into a new category but negative associations with this new category could erode the Core Brand Equity. An example is when a brand owner extends into a new category but that new category does not actually reinforce the position of the core category. If this happens the core category equity can erode which can hurt the overall success of the brand. These are very important considerations to resolve before thinking about extending brands via licensing.

For Brand Extensions to be effective, it is important to follow a couple guidelines. First: Ask yourself, does the brand have the permission to extend into a new category? What I mean by permission is, are consumers willing to see the brand extend into this particular category, and does the category make sense to the consumer? To answer this question market research must be conducted that will uncover what consumers are saying. Consumers are open to tell about their experience with the brand and whether or not an extension in this category strengthens the core brand. Second: Select possible new categories based on core brand equities and similarity in extensions. Do not, I repeat, do not try to extend the brand into an area that does not make sense to the core brand equities. As a brand owner, it is important to consider the Brand Expansion Point whenever looking for new Category Extensions. The reason why this is so important is that, if a brand is placed in a category that does not coincide with the Brand Expansion Point, it will most likely fail in that extension, resulting in a loss of resources. Third: Evaluate the potential of a new category to create equity according to three factors:

- Salience of brand associations
- Favorability of associations inferred by extension
- Uniqueness of associations from the new category

If the salience, favorability, and uniqueness are all in place then there is an opportunity to extend effectively via licensing. Sources such as macro trends, consumer insights and your marketing assessment will help you determine whether to extend the brand.

Another thing you should consider is the amount of benefits that can be attributed to the brand's equity by extension. What are the possible competitive advantages the brand brings from a consumer's perspective? If you have insight to know what the competitive advantages are going to be, that will help to determine whether or not the extensions are going to be successful. Again, consider the Mr. Clean example where the brand extended from the cleaning liquid to the Mr. Clean mop. The Mr. Clean brand is such a powerful brand it makes the mop more competitive in the marketplace versus its competitors. Brand owners should also evaluate new category success and their effects on the Parent Brand Equity. You want to make sure that extension will strengthen the Parent Brand and not erode its equity. This will make the whole program sustainable and increase its overall success in the marketplace.

Understanding how to attract, generate, and screen opportunities allows you to create decision criteria for where to extend the brand.

1. Knowing the brand's position and expansion point assists you in researching the categories from which the brand can be extended. Once a clear Brand Positioning is articulated and the research is completed, you must then determine the attractiveness of the categories. Once completed, ranked them from most to least attractive. You should then examine macro trends, gather consumer insight, do market assessments, and investigate any new and relevant technology to determine whether the priority should be adjusted.

2. Inventions often lead to new technological advances. These can be created by individuals or through a company's R&D department. These technological inventions create intellectual property that can benefit a brand and place it in a position to be license-able. This, in turn, enables the brand licensing the technology to extend into new categories they would not otherwise be able to reach.

3. Another way to evaluate possible Brand Extensions is to ask consumers

4. Brainstorming ways to extend the brand is yet another method.

Each of these methods will help you come up with some great examples. This will make the licensing program more robust.

To gain a better understanding of how all of this information works together in one cohesive unit, let's review a case where this material come to life.

# Penley Case Study

Steve Penley is a renowned artist for Americana art, florals, and landscapes who has painted hundreds of paintings. Take a moment to look at Steve Penley's painting of President Lincoln. Recognizing President Lincoln's face is effortless, because it is a familiar picture that has been seen in many history books and U.S. currency. However, it has probably never been seen with the colors that have been used by Penley. This is what makes him, as an artist, so unique and is why his product, which is his art, is perfectly suited to be extended into licensing through

*Abe 2 created by Steve Penley*

a variety of categories. Although, before executing a licensing program, the Brand Positioning has to be identified. It is imperative to always start with the Brand Positioning before moving forward with any other step. So, let's think about that.

A mission statement is the basis of Brand Positioning and every brand owner is encouraged to create a mission statement to explain what the brand is set out to do. Penley's mission statement states:

"I have chosen uncomplicated subjects such as historical icons because they are something we all have in common. Each of these subjects has meanings which are imprinted in the back of our minds. By manipulating these images, I hope to bring the viewer into a new way of seeing familiar subjects... These formal and sometimes stoic images are a great contrast with bright colors and expressionistic brush strokes. And, hopefully this will give familiar subjects new life."
– Steve Penley

After reading Penley's mission statement the Essence of The Brand is easily recognizable. Penley's art celebrates Americana, it inspires action, it seeks out beauty and vibrancy, and it commemorates heroes and icons. All of these components are why Americans, and even people outside of the United States, want to consume this brand through apparel, tabletop, stationery, and other categories. Being able to bring his art into their homes and into their lives opens the door of opportunity that consumers have been craving. For Steve Penley not to take advantage of this opportunity would be irrational.

When examining the Brand Architecture of the Steve Penley program, start first with the physical attributes, more specifically how his product is constructed. Penley's pieces of art are always of the highest quality, precision made, and created with sustainable materials that preserve the art. Therefore, when entering these categories, the extended products must emulate or align with its architecture. Another attribute to look at is the functional benefits of his products. Steve Penley's branded merchandise has to be exceptionally constructed which means it will be durable and innovative. Penley is creating three-dimensional pieces that not too many other artists are currently doing. It is essential that this same kind of innovation is reflected in his licensed merchandise.

While functional benefits center on the product, emotional benefits focus on how the product connects with the consumer on an emotional level. For the Penley brand, it is essential that the emotional elements connect with the consumer. Mainly because once consumers develop a personal relationship with a brand, they are driven to purchase more products and ultimately become brand loyalists. Penley's brand is about passion, inspiration, uniqueness, and assuredness. The consumer, who wants to feel these emotions, is going to buy Steve Penley licensed merchandise if the product aligns with his paintings. The last threshold is what is termed "the higher order brand identity": What is the something bigger the brand offers? What does the Penley brand bring to the marketplace? This is the unlimited potential. Steve Penley has taking something very ordinary and made it extraordinary. Can you see the potential that he has in his art and merchandise, and how it lends itself to the consumer? What has just been described is the Brand Architecture Draft created for Steve Penley.

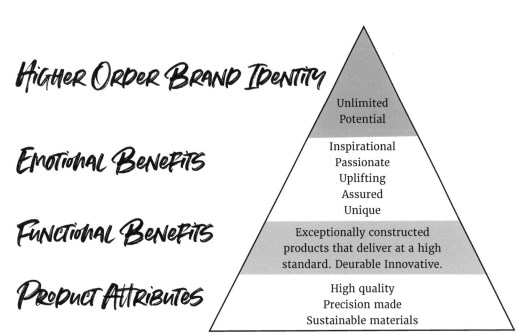

## Penley Art Brand Architecture Draft

*Figure 4-1 Penley Art Brand Architecture Draft*

If you notice the Brand Architecture Pyramid, one aspect can't be produced without the other. It is a constant build that is critical to any program or extension of a program. This Brand Positioning statement about the Penley art merchandise emphasizes how important Brand Positioning is to any Brand Extension program:

> "For Americans who love their country and are proud of its heroes, icons and institutions that have made it great and who wish to be inspired, uplifted and assured, Penley branded merchandise delivers products that celebrate Americana by offering bold, vibrant and powerful images and colors that evoke inspiration, pride and rejuvenation because only Penley branded merchandise avails of Steve Penley art is made with the highest quality materials."
> – Pete Canalichio

Use this Brand Positioning Statement as a Litmus test or a screen for any product that is created with Steve Penley branded merchandise in the marketplace. If those positioning standards are adhered to, success will follow because of the success Penley has had with his art.

Since the Brand Essence and Brand Position are now determined, the category selection process can take place. Before Steve Penley's brand can extend, we had to conduct market research. Consumers who purchased Steve Penley art were asked: In what categories do you expect to see the Steve Penley brand extend? What would you be willing to pay for these products? Where do you expect to buy them? Finally, is there any promotional channel you would expect to see the product? Once the data was collected, we used it to determine where to take the program. Some of the research revealed the most popular categories involved art re-prints. Many consumers love Steve Penley. Unfortunately, not everyone can afford a $10,000 painting. This is why art re-prints are such a popular category for the Steve Penley brand. Even if consumers can't afford a painting, they can afford a reprint that is similar to the real painting. Sometimes Penley will sign the re-print making it even more valuable. The brand also fits nicely into categories such as apparel, stationary, bags, and totes that consumers are will to purchase primarily online.

The implications of the insights we learned from the research teach us that certain categories are likely to be more successful than other categories. The categories that provide a better likelihood of success are the ones that the brand owner should start with. An important component to any successful program is to build awareness. We felt confident we could build awareness of the licensed product through Penley's website, social media, art galleries, and other channels where his paintings are currently sold.

Regarding where to place the product, we felt high-end boutiques would be the best place to start. However, we wanted to move down to mid-tier and potentially even lower channels to achieve Penley's goal of sharing his art with as many people as possible. While the volume may be less, the margin will be higher in the upstairs channels. As time progresses and the Steve Penley brand makes its way to lower channels, the volume should increase while the margins decrease. This is one of the core components of a successful program because of the volume adjustments; the financial aspect of it will still be solid.

Notice that the categories chosen weren't at random. The Brand Essence, Brand Positioning, and extensive research had to be conducted before selecting any categories to extend into. Also, every category that was chosen had to reinforce the Brand Positioning. Each of these components works together to make the brand licensing program a long-term success. If a brand owner tries to select "Where To Play" before completing all the criteria chance are the extensions will fail and valuable resources will be lost.

For Steve Penley our recommendation would be to launch the brand in the categories that were determined through the research. Once the brand is established there then other categories can be considered. Merchandise sales should occur through the website, Penley's Facebook account, specialty stores, and upstairs channels like Saks, Neiman or Nordstrom.

That's the summary of our findings and completes this part of the case studying. Hopefully you have a greater understanding of how we determine "Where To Play" and the success of the Brand Extension program.

# Chapter 5

# How to Win

In the 8-Step Brand Licensing Process, determining "How to Win" is the second step in building a brand licensing program. In this stage of the process, you, the brand owner, will discover there is more to having a successful licensing program than just identifying "Where to Play." This chapter informs you on how to take the foundational elements and collected data associated with step 1, identifying "Where to Play," and devise a strategy on how to go about executing the extension.

When determining "How to Win," the first questions you must answer is: What new categories does our brand have permission to enter and what are the consumers' expectations for brands entering those new categories? Make sure market research backs this answer and do not base your decision on a "guesstimate." If a definite answer is not available, refer back to "Identify Where to Play". This step will help in identifying a majority of foundational aspects including determining which categories the brand has permission to enter. However, if you are able to answer these two questions with relative ease and have the market research to back up the claim, then you are in a good place to move forward. Take a minute to write a list that displays your strengths versus the competitors' strengths. Having a list that is viewable can offer a better understanding of what kind of challenges you may face moving forward. Once all of these elements have been defined, the **Go-To-Market Options**, also known as tactics, can now be taken into consideration.

# Go to Market Options (Tactics)

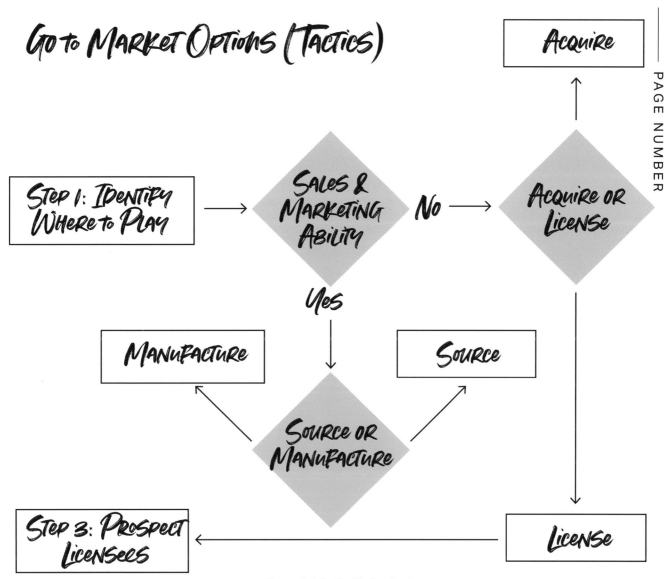

*Figure 5-1 Go-To-Market Options*

In the Go-To-Market Options phase, a series of questions must be answered to determine what tactics would benefit the brand the best. Since you have already identified where to play, the next logical step would be to examine the Sales and Marketing Capabilities. Look at the organization internally to determine whether it is capable of selling and marketing the extended products. If it is, then figure out a process of how to do this internally by answering the following questions:

- Do we currently market and sell our own products?
- Will the new categories selected be sold in the same markets or channels?

- Are the current products and extensions complementary?
- Can they be packaged together?

If the answers to all of these questions are "yes" then you can choose to market and sell the products yourself. However, you are not required to take this route. There may be several reasons why you would choose one course over another. One example is that you may want to save the resources you have to allocate them to other areas of the organization. Even though the opportunity may be presented for you to market and sell the products internally, the question posed is: Does our organization have the ability to manufacture the new product category? If not, how much investment and time will it take to set up the manufacturing for the new product and are we considering sourcing the product? Also, is the product patent protected to be used to our benefit? If you don't have the capability to market and sell products internally or extend into a particular category, but still wants to enter the category, there are two options to choose from. The first is to acquire a company that has the capability to manufacture, market and sell the product. The second is to license a third-party manufacturer to extend the brand through that route.

Questions you want to ask yourself when deciding whether to acquire a company or license a third-party manufacture are:

- Do we have the financial resources to acquire a company?
- If we have the resources, is it a paramount that we own the supply chain?
- If we have the resources would we rather use the capital for something else?

Most likely if you have the financial resources to acquire a company you can go this route, but you may choose to use your resources in another capacity. The big picture for you to keep in mind at this juncture is that financial resources provide the option to acquire a company. If you are considering acquiring a company, but capital is needed for R&D (Research and Development), marketing and promotion, or to buy another company, you can choose to delay purchase and use licensing as an alternative as it enables you to use your capital for other priorities. Ultimately the decision to acquire a company or license the brand falls upon you as the brand owner. Neither choice is better than the other, but make sure that the decision made benefits the brand and does not harm the organization financially. Now that the decision matrix is completed, you have a choice of whether or not to license.

Once you have made a decision to take the licensing route, the next phase of the process is prospecting suitable manufacturers to license your brand in order for it to enter the market. Brand licensing can build your Brand's Equity because it provides a repeatable and scalable strategic platform for growth; that's important to any company. Assuming that it can be repeated while using minimal resources, and is scalable, then licensing can grow the brand in a variety of ways and the resources needed for other priorities that are core to the business are made available. By third-party manufacturing through licensing, new channels and markets become open. The reason for that is current and potential partners already have relationships in those channels or markets. This can be tremendously beneficial, considering how hard it can be to get into a new channel or new markets. Having a partner who has already developed a relationship with other vendors or retailers, who has that capability to manufacture, market, and produce the product, is a much more efficient way to go. What else does licensing do? It minimizes your risk while maximizing their return. How? By using best-in-class, experienced partnerships that have knowledge about your core business and are excellent in what they do. Additionally, no inventory has to be bought. The third-party manufacturer assumes the costs associated with the inventory, keeping your cost to a minimum. Finally, in this particular area, little or no staff is required since the third-party manufacturer is responsible for everything from R&D through production, marketing, and sales. Your only responsibility is managing the Approval Process as it relates to the brand being used on the licensed product.

There are also some intangible benefits associated with brand licensing that include: marketing support, brand insights, and knowledge transfer. Marketing support takes place when a third- party manufacturer needs to dedicate a portion of their business to marketing the brand. This is very valuable for you in a sense that marketing support can potentially double the entire marketing effort. For instance, let's assume you allocate a percentage of your budget to marketing for one of your core set of products. Likewise, manufacturers who are your licensing partners, are also allocating a portion of their business to marketing their core products while they are extending your brand into dozens of categories. Due to an extensive amount of marketing the percentages of the sales completed might equal or even surpass your own investment in marketing. Henceforth, potentially doubling your marketing effort. Knowledge transfer can go both ways, so it's beneficial for both parties. As you build relationships with manufacturers that are excellent in R&D, promotions, and sales; this knowledge gets transferred to you and vice-versa. The transference builds a much better relationship between the parties and creates a stronger chance of winning in the future.

By extending brands through licensing, you're allowed to continue to do what you do best which is to focus on your core business. This allows other companies to do what they do best which is their core business while also providing the consumers with your brand in the categories that it has the permission to enter. This is one of the most important aspects of this technique. Identifying the right categories and the right partners to extend the brand into is critical, irrespective of the Go-To-Market Options strategy, but if using it for brand licensing it is going to be core to the success of your program.

How should you Prioritize Options? Look at the biggest opportunities. These are evaluated in what is affectionately called the *Size of The Prize*. Now how big is the size of the prize? How big is the market and how big is our share in the market going to be? There may be a great opportunity to extend into a category that's needed in the marketplace, but if the Size of The Prize is small then that opportunity is going to be placed lower on the priority list. What are our internal competencies? Internal competencies allow you to have more decisions about how you Go-To-Market. Those competencies can allow you to manufacture the product internally, or source the product and then market and sell it. If you don't possess these competencies than you would have to acquire a company or license the brand. Collectively this gives you a number of choices. Knowing your internal competences is critical to making the best choice. For example, what cash resources do we have available? Are we like the Coca-Cola Company who has $10B of cash or cash equivalents? Or, are we strapped for cash and need to use the cash we have in another way that is more important? This is an important consideration and an important question for you to answer. Then what are the Optimal Tactics for exploiting the opportunities? Think about your decision on how you will go to market based on the competencies, cash availability, and resources; then determine what prioritization is needed. Finally compare against the Size of The Prize to Prioritize Options.

What extensions are you going to execute through licensing? Suppose there are ten choices. You may say: "1-5 is through our own manufacturing, 6-7 are through sourcing, 8 is through acquisition and 9-10 are through licensing." Then you need to find best-in-class manufacturers in categories nine and ten and allow them to execute the licensing program. By the way, that's not necessarily based on Size of The Prize. It actually may be that 9-10 are your biggest opportunities in the marketplace to connect with the most consumers. It's just the prioritization process.

That completes Chapter 5, "How to Win." We are looking forward to jumping into the next chapter, which is about "Prospecting Licensees."

# CHAPTER 6
# Prospect Licensees

Once a product category that qualifies for Brand Extension has been identified, and you, the licensor has chosen brand licensing as the preferred method to achieve this extension, then it is time to scout for prospective licensees within the selected product category. Selecting the most suitable licensee can be a daunting task for any licensor to accomplish, but don't worry, help has come! In this section, "Prospect Licensees," you will learn how to cultivate a pool of qualified companies for further evaluation.

To understand which licensees will help in accomplishing the brand licensing goal the licensor must first understand what makes a best-in-class licensee. Knowing what separates a lousy licensee from one that is best-in-class allows licensors to avoid choosing licensees that will not meet expectations and potentially diminish the brand. Best-in-class licensees are those who:

- Believe in the vision of the brand and see the benefit of establishing the brand in their category
- Understand consumer needs and are willing to invest in marketing
- Has demonstrated success in the marketplace and achieved category captain status
- Have strong leadership and are well managed
- Possess excellent references from licensors and retailers
- Focus on innovation and product development
- Deliver consistent financial results

When you find licensees with best-in-class attributes and extend your brand through those licensees the likelihood of a successful brand licensing program is high. Being aware of the attributes of best-in-class licensees provides you with a template for what type of prospective licensee will help to support and carry the brand towards success. The definition of the word prospect is to "search or explore a region for a particular item". In our case, we want a partner who can successfully extend the brand into the marketplace. Once the prospects are selected an evaluation takes place to determine how successful they will be moving forward.

Like anything else that's of value there is often times an art component and a *science component* in that evaluation process. The science component measures and examines the statistics side that evolves the operations of the partnership. For example, what's the licensee's leadership? Are they a category captain? Do they show financial consistency in the marketplace? Do they grow over time? Do they care about the insights that they are picking up and using those insights in product development? Do they invest in marketing? Whereas the art component is about understanding how the licensee fits with the organization. Is the chemistry the same? Do they believe the same things philosophically that the licensor believes? Are they a hungry company that is going to do things the right way and not get dragged down by challenges, but rather look at those challenges and opportunities to succeed? When both the science and art components conjoin and integrate the best-in-class licensee, a program is set up to be successful in the marketplace. Considering all these factors, how can one find the right prospects? Through four selection techniques: Research, Trade Publications, Store Walks, and Trade Shows. Let's talk about each selection technique in more detail.

**Research** can be conducted independently or through a third-party. Regardless of the route selected it is critical to research to understand who the players are and their qualities. When investigating, a company's website can be a tremendous resource for finding out about the company. Many prospects have gone through the trouble of detailing their mission and vision as well as their financial success if they are a public company. A tremendous amount of information can be gathered from their public relations releases, so start there. Learn as much as possible through their websites then

*Subscription Bases Online Providers of Information; Source: Google Images*

view online business directories such as Manta to help find other information about those companies or other companies of interest. Portals such as Yahoo Finance provide extensive background information about a particular company. Other supplementary Information such as a particularly new innovation that is going to impact the success of the company may also be found. There are other sources that are helpful, including Hoovers, Datamonitor, or Factiva. Now, these are subscription-based online providers of information, but it's well worth spending the money to have that subscription to get the insights that they devote full time trying to capture. Therefore, make sure to do the research. Getting the information needed is the first component of this process.

*Published Directory; Sources: Google Images*

**Trade publications** are another type of source to use when finding potential prospects. Search for publications that have spent a tremendous amount of investment learning about the makers in the marketplace. Trade publications make a living by knowing about their industry inside and out so dig deep into those trade publications for the category chosen to learn about who is manufacturing that category. Observe who are the best in class manufacturers? What kind of innovation is upcoming? What are their leadership characteristics? Then brainstorm about what other information can be learned about them? Maybe there is some subtleties about whether or not they are in trouble from a liability perspective that must be known. Lastly in the licensing industry there are several companies that produce published directories. A company called Kazachok is one of many companies that creates published directories. This company is based in Paris and has a number of companies in their directory for France and greater Europe. Other useful directories include Toy Directory, Baby and Children's, HFN, and Licensing Intelligence. Take time to review these directories and dig into them. The more time a licensor devotes to reviewing these publications, the more information and resources they will receive to find desirable licensees. Once the right prospects are found, success will follow.

Licensors should also consider **Store Walks**. Licensors should go to stores where they expect to see their brand sold then discover who is making those products in the categories they want to license. Finding the manufacturer is as simple as picking up the product off the shelf and reading the information on the label on the back of the packaging. If your brand is a mid or lower tier brand, then move into retail stores that mirror the brand and look in the departments where the product is sold. For example, if you represent the Rubbermaid brand and you want to sell licensed garden hoses then go to a Home Depot, Target or Walmart and browse the gardening section to find out who is manufacturing hoses. Find out which hoses best emulate the brand's equities and find out who are the manufacturers. That's the kind of extremely valuable information licensors can obtain through a store walk. After the information is gathered, go back and do the research as a follow up to what was discovered before to reveal more information about those particular companies.

The last option for finding prospective licensees is at **Trade Shows**. Even though a licensor might not be interested in trade shows it is an important place to go find prospects. Trade shows will generally have a much higher audience of prospects than a licensor will see in a store walk. When I managed Rubbermaid's global licensing business, we went to the Homewares Show, the Housewares Show, and the Gourmet Show, to find best in class manufacturers to be potential licensees. Oftentimes manufacturers are not thinking about becoming a licensee, they are thinking about how they can sell their product to prospective customers, but it's fertile ground for a licensor to find them. Using a combination of all four selection techniques should give the licensor a robust list of prospective companies in which to license the business.

After spotting and cataloging several prospective licensees using the selection techniques, it is time to develop a basic checklist of **parameters** to evaluate them. Parameters include:

**Geographic Reach:** Consider the geographic reach when examining a licensee. Are they selling in the region the licensor is in or want to be in? If not, even though the licensee may be best-in- class, they are not a suitable candidate for the licensor. Having a licensee that is already established in the region the mirrors where the brand is strong and wants to be sold eliminates many unforeseen issues for a prospective licensee that does not have this distribution.

**Service:** Are service levels high? You must research this information to accurately rate how well the licensee is servicing their customers. For instance, if you conduct a store walk and discovers a bunch of empty shelves, then the licensee is not servicing their customers, as they should.

**Financial Health:** Locating the financial health of public companies is relatively easy to find, but for private companies it is much more difficult. Subscribing to services like Hoovers and Datamonitor are very important in determining the overall financial health of private companies. Once the licensee is selected and they agree to be considered a part of the brand licensing program, you can request financial statements from them to address any concerns you may have.

**Continuous Improvement:** Are the licensees interested in continuous improvement? Analyzing the licensees' history of innovation provides an overview of where they started and where they're going. If they have a track record of making refinements, filing patents and improving their products features and benefits then that is a good indication of future success.

**Product Scope:** Is their product scope broad or narrow? Depending on the category selected, having a narrow scope may be suitable for you. Although oftentimes a broader scope is preferred.

**Capacity:** What is manufacturing capacity of the prospective licensee? Are they going to able to handle the brand's demand in the present channels? If many enjoy the brand, one can assume that demand for the product will increase substantially. To meet this demand the licensee must be ready to make a substantial investment. Moreover, they must have the right distribution system in place to reach consumers.

**History**: What is the company's history? Are they licensed with other brands? If so, who? It is imperative to understand where the organizations started, where they are now, and how they got there. Make sure to focus on whether or not they have had a history of market success.

**Channel Reach**: Are the prospective licensees selling in the channels that we desire? Do they have a category captain status in that particular channel? If so, then you know they are going to have a better chance of success.

**Price**: Does their pricing aligned with our pricing? Is it low-tier, mid-tier, high-tier? How does the licensee's prices compare with our price? Are they aligned?

| Parameters | Licensors Expectations |
|---|---|
| Geographic Reach | Extensive |
| Service | High |
| Financial Health | Strong |
| Innovation | Strong |
| Continuous Improvement | Ongoing |
| Quality | High |
| Product Scope | Broad |
| Capacity | Available |
| History | Market Success |
| Channel Reach | Broad |
| Price | Aligned with Channel |

*Figure 6-1 Parameters and Expectations*

This completes the assessment check that you need to make once you have identified those prospective licensees. The check will enable you to hone down the list of candidates that are going to be best suited for your brand.

Once the checklist is established, the next step is to interview the licensee. This is in many ways similar to a job interview. The licensor contacts the licensee through phone calls, meetings or e- mails to assess their level of interest. The prospective licensee may not be contemplating licensing a brand, but if the licensor has a best-in-class brand that is desirable, contact may peak their interest and lead to the next step in the brand licensing process. To summarize, the first step for the licensor is to identify the prospective licensees. Selection techniques such as Research, Store Walks, Trade Shows, Trade Publications allow you to locate potential candidates. The next step is to make a checklist of parameters to evaluate. These include the prospects history of success, interest in the marketplace, overall breadth of sales in the region and in a channel. Their level of success and fit with the brand will help you determine if the licensee has the potential to be a qualified partner. If so, complete an evaluation to assess their interest level. Lastly take that interested parties to the next step, "Performing Due Diligence".

## Chapter 7

# Perform Due Diligence

"Performing Due Diligence" is step four of the 8-Step Brand Licensing Process. In Chapter 6, "Prospect Licensees," we took you through the process of finding and selecting prospective licensees for further evaluation. In this Due Diligence stage, you begin rigorously qualifying the prospective licensees to determine whether they will progress to the next phase. To complete this Due Diligence phase three areas are emphasized. These include: a) points to consider, b) separating the curious from the serious, and c) areas for evaluation. Toward the end of this chapter, the licensor should ideally be left with two to three qualified candidates. Let's begin.

Four points to consider when **Performing Due Diligence** phase are the Objectives, Strategic Considerations, Financial Considerations, and Legal Considerations. The objectives work as a measuring tool to see which licensees achieve the brand's goals.

**Objectives** to consider are the following:

- Stimulate profitable long-term growth of licensing revenues. The right partner in place will enable this to happen; the wrong partner will ultimately lead to failure.
- Maximize the efficiency and effectiveness of the licensing teams. Ask, who are the players on that team? How do they marry up with the players on our team?
- Eliminate major risk. Are the partners considered in a position of liability? If so, even if they have other strengths, this may be a disqualifying factor.
- Ensure that the right controls are in place. This precaution permits success in the marketplace

Under the heading of **Strategic Considerations**, Brand Equity Protection is critical. You have built the brand's value over time so, it is crucial that the brand is never put in a position of compromise. Therefore, taking the provided steps in this Due Diligence section protects the brand. In addition to preserving the Brand Equity it is important to ensure fair compensation can be expected from the program based on a segment or category value. If the potential partner is capable of extending the brand to its fullest capacity in the category you want than you should be in good shape. If not, they may not be qualified. Think about it from an opportunity perspective. If your brand should be in three or four major channels in three- quarters of a specific region of the world, then you need to uncover who can successfully get the brand in the marketplace, in those channels, and in those regions. The challenge is to find those particular partners you believe are capable and to evaluate them to make sure of your decision.

From a **Financial Considerations** perspective, it is important to review a company at a microeconomic level. To do this, consider implications of Sarbanes Oxley and GAAP (Generally Accepted Accounting Principles). Once you have done this, you will obtain a picture of the financial strength of each prospective company. It's not just about whether or not you can pay the Royalty Revenue. It's about whether or not you are going to be in business long after the relationship ends. How about the deal quality? Licensors will reflect on aspects like the financial arrangement:

- How well do they forecast the risk?
- What procedures do they take to protect themselves?
- Are they going to be solvent long after the relationship ends?
- Can they timely execute the programs they are talking about putting forward?
- Are we going to have a good deal or a bad deal if we partner with this perspective licensee?

Then discuss the P&L treatment across divisions and the company. Make sure the Due Diligence is done well enough that an understanding of the Royalty Revenue to be earned is received and judiciously disseminated across the company.

**Legal Considerations** are vital elements to comprehend before entering a partnership. There are certain required standards in the marketplace, and it is essential for you to know if the prospective licensees will be able to comply with the legal standards. This is especially critical when dealing with products that are in the children's space, since the criteria and the legal standards are extremely high. Be mindful of how robust of a legal contract you are going to have with the licensee. Make sure to consider all the different legal scenarios that can cause harm to the brand and strategize to protect it. Take the time to create a strong contract that the partner is willing to sign. Finally, what kind of Due Diligence are we implementing to make sure that from a legal perspective we are protected?

***

Next, you must start separating the *curious* from the *serious*. A thorough application will help accomplish this. If you select a prospective licensee who shows initial interest, but then loses that interest after you send them the application, they are most likely more *curious* than *serious*. Other characteristics that you could consider as curious behavior might include the licensee balking at the questions they are asked and their taking an extended period of time getting back with you to secure the deal. They are not serious about entering the market with your brand in this channel. If they were, they would be forthrightly completing the process; they would look at it as any request for proposal, and they would put resources behind it to get you, the licensor, the information you need. Assuming your brand is terrific, it deserves an extensive application to be completed in order for the licensee to tell you how they are going to accomplish what they say. The ones that complete the application in a timely fashion are the serious licensees who are interested in acquiring a license.

***

As a brand owner, you must evaluate different areas of a licensee to gain a

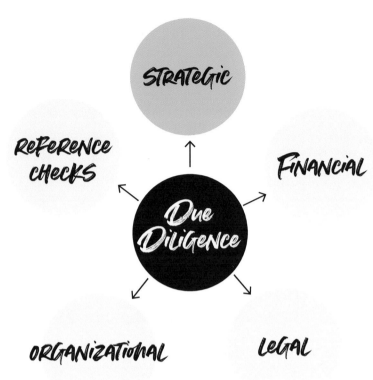

better understanding of who they are and if they are qualified prospects. There are five different areas for evaluation to consider in continuation of the due diligence process. The first is strategic. In the **Strategic Stage** you want to know that the licensee clearly understands both the consumers and the brand. As well as have a strong product development, understand and value the importance of market research, have strong advertising and promotion budget, and allocates the right level of percentage of their P&L to this category.

While in this stage a) assess that their leadership is strong, b) they believe in your brand, and c) they can deliver on what they say they are going to accomplish. You can even use the Category Captain designation as a measurement of their leadership along with the relationships they have developed with retailers and their channel presence. When investigating the manufacturers' relationships talk to the buyers, marketing directors, and the retailers to gain a perception of what kind of company in which you are about to enter a relationship. Then reference their channel presence to see if they have an extensive presence with "40 feet of shelf space" in the category or do they have "2 feet of shelf space." Look at their innovation capabilities. Are they constantly coming out with new technology and new products or do they still rely on old technology that they developed decades ago? Once you have a good strategic understanding of the business, then start evaluating their financial strength.

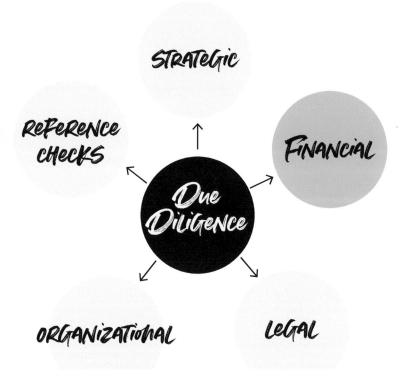

**Financial Strength** is the second area for evaluation. Begin by examining your D&B (Dun & Bradstreet) reports. D&B evaluates companies' financial risk on a regular basis. Make sure the scores that the license receives meet your minimum standards and exceed them in most cases. Next, conduct credit references. Talk to agencies that evaluate credit for companies and learn if the company you are considering has good credit and has strong bank references. You may not get all the details of their bank relationship or banking accounts, but the bank can tell you whether or not the company is strong financially. After you have gathered a good amount of financial knowledge on the manufacturer go directly to them and ask for their financial statements. Many times, these companies are private and don't want to give up their financial statements, but if they want to license your brand they will have to provide you with their financial information. If they choose not to then you may not want to partner with them.

The third area of evaluation to consider is the **Legal Risk** perspective. Ask the manufacturer about any past lawsuits

or pending lawsuits; this is critical information that you need to know. Be adamant that they be forthcoming in telling you what happened, why it happened, and what they did to mitigate or absorb the problem. The same goes for pending lawsuits. (The licensee likely will have you sign a nondisclosure agreement before they share this information with you.) It is critical that you know what kind of risk you are exposing your brand to. For example, if the licensee is a ladder company, and they have a pending lawsuit because somebody slipped off their ladder and got killed, you need to know that. Even if they are not at fault, you need to know what is going on. Additionally, know the level of due diligence as it relates to how they deal with their vendors. This information should be openly shared with you.

**Organizational Competency** is the fourth area of evaluation to consider. How well is the company managed? Do they have strong leadership that's been in place for a long time or have they changed their CEO four times in the last ten years? What kind of structure do they have? Are they set up structurally to reinforce and extend your brand in an optimal fashion? Or are they haphazard in their structure and are potentially going to limit the success of your program? Are they internally aligned? Do they see the same way that you do about your brand? And lastly what kind of cultural fit do they have? Do they think like you do or not? These are great questions to ask as you determined how the company's leadership is managed, structured, aligned, and whether it fits with yours culturally.

The last area evaluation for you to complete is the **Licensors References**. If a licensee has multiple licenses with other licensors you want to get the contact information of those licensors to call them and ask them questions like:

- How's their product quality?
- What does their product development look like?
- How well do they design?
- Do they have strong sales and marketing capability?
- What kind of success are they having with your license?

If the manufacturers' references are strong and the licensing program with other brands is strong then this is the best indication of future success. Other components that you should review are their service ability. How well is the product getting into the marketplace? How strong are they on packaging? What's their payment history like? Do they pay on time? Do they meet their business planning and forecasting? Are they engaging with you or they inactive in getting the information you need? What's their customer service like? Is it easy to find an "800" number on their website? If yes, you should call that number to evaluate them. When you call the customer service number, how do they respond? Or, how do they follow up on the e-mail? Pretend you are the customer and see how they respond. That's the kind of reference check you need to be conducting.

For **Buyer References** get to know the names of the buyers from the retailers in which they are planning to sell their licensed product. Talk to these buyers about the success the prospective licensee has had. In this step, you want to ask the same types of questions are about their product quality, service levels, marketing, pricing, category leadership, product innovation, warranty, and returns. Get the information you need to know regardless if the licensee is best- in-class or mediocre. Once you have all that information and all those reference checks are conducted, you will have a great understanding of whether or not these prospective licensees are going to meet your criteria and be successful in the marketplace.

Here is an example where we have four prospective licensees in the home ladders category. I will be portraying the brand owner who is going to ask the prospective licensee questions and record their answers. I'm going to evaluate them based on the criteria listed below.

## Market Share Rankings
Prospect A ranks 3rd
Prospect B ranks 1st
Prospect C ranks 4th
Prospect D ranks 2nd

### What channels are they in?

Prospect A and B are in the mass channel

Prospect C is in the department store channel

Prospect D is in mass and department stores

### Financial strength?

Prospect A has medium financial strength

Prospect B is strong

Prospect C is strong

Prospect D is strong

### What other licenses are held in the category?

Prospect A has none

Prospect B has the Black & Decker license

Prospect C has no licenses, prospect

Prospect D has the Stanley license

### What is the product innovation capability?

Prospect A none that we know of

Prospect B is innovative

Prospect C is innovative

Prospect D is innovative.

## WHO WOULD YOU PICK?

| | Prospect A | Prospect B | Prospect C | Prospect D |
|---|---|---|---|---|
| **Market share rank in category** | 3 | 1 | 4 | 2 |
| **Channels** | Mass merchants | Mas merchants | Department Stores | Mass merchants, Department Stores |
| **Financial Strength** | Medium | Strong | Strong | Strong |
| **Offer lincenses held in category** | None | Black & Decker | None | Stanley |
| **Product innovation capability** | No | Yes | Yes | Yes |

*Figure 7-1 Prospective Licensees Case Study Chart*

Based on the information provided I'm going to eliminate Prospect A first. They are third in market share, only have one channel of access, are medium in financial strength, and have no other licenses or innovation. Choices B, C, and D are still the running for now. If I look at Prospect C, I know that they are fourth in market share, so that concerns me somewhat, although fourth is still not a bad place to be. However, they don't have any other licenses, and relative to Prospects B and C they are the weakest of the three and so I'll eliminate them. Now I'm left with B and D. Prospect B ranks number one and Prospect D is number 2; they are very comparable. At this point, I want to know the difference between the levels of market share. If prospect 1 is 50 percent of the market and prospect 2 is only 25 percent that is going to weigh in my decision. Looking at the channels, I know that Prospect B is only in the mass channel and Prospect D is in mass and department stores channels. If I have a mid-tier brand that is sold primarily in mid-tier department stores and less so in the mass channel, that is going to help me determine whether or not I choose Prospect B or Prospect D. Both prospects are financially strong so I feel comfortable about that. They both have great licenses. One is with Black & Decker and one is with Stanley; they are both strong brands and we know that they are both innovative. Without any other information, and taking into consideration that Prospect D is just one rank lower than Prospect B in market share, I'm going to choose Prospect D. The deciding factor was the channel criteria. Prospect D was already operating in the mass and department store channels. I could have selected Prospect B for the reasons I mentioned, but Prospect D would benefit the brand in that one area that Prospect B couldn't. These are the kinds of questions you should be asking and answering before you decide which company you are going to select.

One additional consideration to include is the quality of the people working on the licensing team or with the agent if applicable that is dealing with this property? What input are we getting from the other departments? For example: What is marketing saying? What is the finance team saying? What is the legal department saying? And, what is senior management saying when we look at all the criteria? As a brand owner, you want your colleagues to weigh in on the decision making process. When collecting data understand the prospective licensees' strengths in each of these different areas: marketing, finance, legal and operations. Also, formulate or acquire an extensive Licensee

Application for the licensees to complete and then sign, confirming that they stand behind the information they provided. The Licensee Application will differentiate the curious from the serious and you'll know that you're dealing with a serious player.

## Summarizing The Process

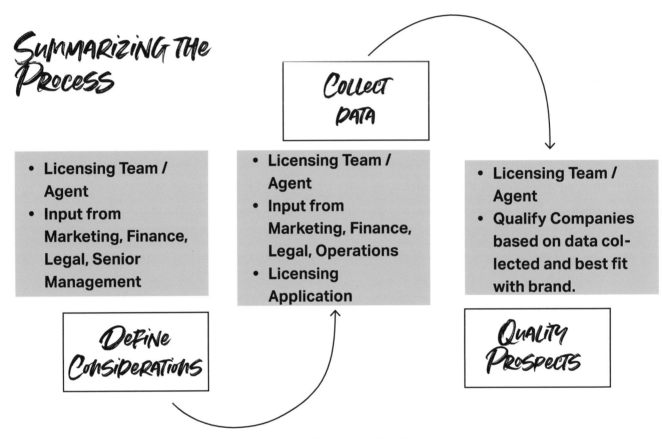

*Figure 7-2 Summarizing The Process*

In conclusion, you want to evaluate the quality of the prospects by the quality of data collected, what the assessments have been, and by each of the reference checks (buyer, licensor, financial and legal). Through this evaluation you will know which of the prospective licensees meet the Due Diligence requirements. These are highly qualified companies to take to the next stage.

# Chapter 8
# Define Licensing Opportunity - Part I

Once the Due Diligence stage is completed, and a qualified licensee has been identified you must define the Licensing Opportunity. This stage contains a hefty amount of material, so it has been broken down into two chapters for easy application. Both Part I and Part II will discuss how to assess the size and the scope of the actual licensed product program. To complete this stage you will need to work with the candidate licensees to understand their strengths and determine whether the licensing opportunity is viable.

What does it mean to Define The Licensing Opportunity? To define a licensing opportunity, you must consider the objective and the desired outcome. The objective, in this particular part of the program, is to scope or "size" the Licensing Opportunity. You want to know how much revenue the opportunity will generate and how it will be derived, i.e. the metrics including regions, retailers and SKUs, so that when you define the Anchor Deal Terms you will be able to formalize the agreement. The desired outcome focuses on the Product Concepts, Initial Sales Forecast, the Licensees' Strengths and Capabilities, and the Deal Parameters.

In Chapter 7, the Licensee Application was introduced and briefly discussed. As we move forward in this phase, the sections included in the Licensee Application will be analyzed on an individual basis. The first section of the Licensee Application lays out the General Information, which is important to know. Questions that should be posed to the prospective licensee in this phase include: What is the legal name of your company? Where are you based? What's your phone number? What's your website address? One major question that absolutely must be included (and answered) in the application is: Who are your corporate officers? These are the people whom you are going to be engaging with if you move forward with them.

# Prospective Licensee Application
*Win a Brand's License by Acing the Application*

## I. General

A.  Legal Company Name: _____

B.  Address: _____

C.  Main Phone: _____

D.  Website: _____

E.  Corporate Officers:

| Name | Phone Number |
|------|--------------|
|      |              |
|      |              |
|      |              |

F. Primary Contacts:

| Name and Title | Phone Number | Email |
|----------------|--------------|-------|
|                |              |       |

When I was running Rubbermaid's Global Licensing program, I typically dealt with the Chief Executive Officer, the Chief Financial Officer, or the Head of Business Development of the prospective licensee. The final question that you should ask is: Who is the primary contact that will be supplying us with the information we request? The licensee will provide a designated contact that you will be able to speak with directly. Ensure that this person is capable of getting you the information you need to evaluate the deal. Don't hesitate to let senior management know if he or she is not.

The next section of the Licensee Application comprises the **Financial Information.** This includes their company sales for the prior three years and an understanding of their Net Worth. When following up on any questions you have regarding this information, ask if they are a public company (whose financial information is relatively easy to gain through public filings) or if they are a private company (whose financial information is typically non-disclosed to outside entities). If the ownership is public, ask them to include their latest annual report; if it private, ask for a list of principal owners. You will also need to get their Federal ID Number and a copy of their Dun & Bradstreet (D&B) report for the company.

## II. Financials
*(Attach annual statements.)*

A. Company sales volume for this year (estimated) and past two years actual:

| 2 Years Ago | Last Year | This Year (estimate) |
|---|---|---|
| $ | $ | $ |

B. Approx. Net Worth of company?  $ _____

C. Ownership:        ☐ Private              ☐ Public

   1) If public, include latest annual report

   2) If private, list principal owners:

| Name |
|---|
|  |

D. Company's Federal ID #: _____

E. Company's D & B #: _____

More financial information requested in the Licensee Application includes their primary bank, the address of the bank and the contact information for the bank. Another important component is their credit references. When you review the credit references provided, check the quality of those credit references and then talk to those credit references and evaluate the prospect's creditworthiness. Similarly, you want them to provide you with the names of the buyers from the primary retailers with whom they anticipate selling your branded product, if you choose to grant them the license. You want to be able to talk to those buyers and find out how well they have been performing. This will give you a strong indication of how well they will perform as your licensee.

F.  Primary Bank:

| Address | |
|---|---|
| Contact / Title | |
| Phone | |

G. Credit References (Three References):

| Contact Name | Phone Number | Fax Number |
|---|---|---|
| | | |
| | | |
| | | |

H.  Buyer References (please list 3 retail buyers we can contact for confidential references:

| Contact Name | Phone Number | Fax Number |
|---|---|---|
| | | |
| | | |
| | | |

Section III of the Licensee Application concentrates on the **Current Products and Brands** that the prospect is selling in the marketplace [What is the estimated percentage in dollar shares of the market for each category?]. By knowing the composition of the prospect's current sales, you will have a good sense of their capability to sell your brand. The application should also require them to list the category of products that they currently sell, the percentage of the market share that category represents, and the equivalent dollar amount. If the prospect intends to sell your brand in their priority category, then they have a better chance of being successful. If the prospective licensee is trying to sell your licensed brand in a category that is a third or fourth priority for their company (based on their sales), then they should be prepared to convince you as to why, e.g. they are preparing to investment in the category based on your brand and make it a higher priority. However, if only 10 percent of their business is in the category that they are intending to license your brand in and 90 percent of it isn't with your brand, you know that their chance of being successful will be low.

## III. Product/Brands

A. Your estimated percent and dollar share of market in each category (define SOM if other than against total category market):

| Category | % Share | $ | |
|----------|---------|---|---|
|          |         | % | $ |
|          |         | % | $ |
|          |         | % | $ |

B. List all brand names under which the company sells its products:

C. Are any of these private or exclusive labels to one or more retailers? If so, which retailers? _____

D. List licenses held and how many years:

| License | Years Held |
|---------|------------|
|         |            |
|         |            |
|         |            |

After the prospect completes the estimated percentage and "dollar share" of the market for each category, have them list the names of the brands they are licensing and using to sell their products. This will help you identify if the prospective licensee has their own in- house brands or other household (licensed) brands and how well those brands are performing? Then, ask the licensee: What licenses do you hold? As a brand owner, you hope that the prospective licensee has several licenses because this will inform you that they have already gone through the "due diligence" process with other licensors. This experience confirms that the prospective licensee has already met a threshold of competence and capability as is evaluated by other major brands in the market choosing to grant them a license. If they don't, it doesn't disqualify them; it just makes your job a bit harder. Furthermore, get information about who the primary contact with each licensed brand is so that you can include them in your evaluation, i.e. interview them to learn more about the prospective licensee. The types of questions to ask are provided in Chapter 7, Due Diligence, as it relates to Licensor References.

E. List the contact information for each licensor:

| | | |
|---|---|---|
| | Primary Contact | |
| | Company | |
| | License | |
| 1 | Address | |
| | Phone | |
| | Email | |

In the **Organization** section, you want to know more about the composition of the prospective licensee's organization. To ensure you receive the appropriate information, ask the prospective licensee to describe the structure of their organization. For instance ask them: "What does your sales team look like? What does your marketing team look like? Can you describe your design and merchandising programs?" These areas are critical components of a successful licensing program and you need to understand how qualified the prospective licensee is in each. Other questions prospective licensees should be asked include: "How well do you distribute your product? Do you have one distribution center for each region or do you have multiple distribution centers?" If you, as the brand owner and prospective licensor, have a national brand that will be successful across a broad region, then it is critical to the success of your licensing program that the prospective licensee be able to get the product distributed across the entire region. In this case multiple distribution centers may be better than one.

# IV. Organization

A. Please describe the company's organization (e.g. how set up, number of employees, etc.):

| | |
|---|---|
| Sales | |
| Marketing | |
| Design / Merchandising | |
| Distribution | |

Ask the prospective licensee to qualify their distribution by channel and to give you a percentage of the sales of the product they are selling in each particular channel. Verify that the percentages align with the channels that you prefer them to sell through. If the prospective licensee has a stronger distribution capability outside of the channels you want them to sell in, then this data will inform you that they may not be as strong as you would like them to be in the channel you prefer. Consider asking follow-up questions such as: "Our brand is strongest in the sports specialty channel and your organization appears to be strongest in the mass channel. How will you ensure that our licensed product will be distributed in an efficient manner to be successful?" The Application's design helps to facilitate the kinds of questions you should ask to determine whether the prospective licensee would be a strong fit with your brand.

B.

| Current Distribution (U.S.) | % Co. Sales | Leading Accounts Sold |
|---|---|---|
| 1. Catalogs | % | |
| 2. Convenience Stores | % | |
| 3. Club Stores | % | |
| 4. Department Stores | % | |
| 5. Discount Stores | % | |
| 6. Drug Stores | % | |
| 7. Food Stores | % | |
| 8. Home / Hardware Stores | % | |
| 9. Houseware Stores | % | |
| 10. Internet | % | |
| 11. National Chains | % | |
| 12. Regional Chains | % | |
| 13. Sporting Goods | % | |
| 14. Toy Stores | % | |
| 15. Wal-Mart / Kmart / Target | % | |
| 16. Other (specify) | % | |

The Licensee Application also requests **Organization** information by region, i.e. on whether the prospective licensee is considering licensing the brand internationally. If this is the case, you should ask the licensee: "What countries do you want to license our brand in? Do you know whether those countries are aligned with our brand trademark protection?" For example, if the prospective licensee desires to license your brand in Europe, you need to ensure your brand is trademark protected in Europe. This means you will have to select only those countries they have competency in and that you also have trademark protection. If the prospective licensee desires to expand your brand regionally and you have trademark protection in those specific regions, this could help expand your global presence.

C. International

List all major countries in which company sells product, each country's share of total company sales volume and major retailers:

| Country | % Share | Retailers |
|---------|---------|-----------|
| 1. | % | |
| 2. | % | |
| 3. | % | |
| 4. | % | |
| 5. | % | |
| 6. | % | |
| 7. | % | |

The **Marketing** section of the Licensee Application will enable you to understand what kinds of advertising the prospective licensee uses to market your brand. Questions listed in the application include: "Are you in national advertising, regional advertising, trade advertising, or a combination? What are the different types of advertising you use? How do these align with our brand?" Trade advertising can be a terrific way to get the word out to prospective business customers, but if your brand is consumer-based you want to know other types of advertising that are going to use to reach consumers. Therefore, it's critical that you understand and convey how much money they are spending against each type of advertising to know whether or not they are positioned to be successful.

# V. Marketing

## A. Advertising/Promotion

Check those areas against which the company spends and what percent of the overall marketing budget each represents:

| | Yes | % Mktg. Budget |
|---|---|---|
| National Consumer Advertising | ☐ | % |
| Regional Consumer Advertising | ☐ | % |
| Trade Advertising | ☐ | % |
| Co-op Advertising | ☐ | % |
| Sponsorship | ☐ | % |
| Endorsements | ☐ | % |
| In-Store Fixturing / Signage | ☐ | % |
| Others (specify): | ☐ | % |

You will then have to ask for their advertising agency contacts to inquire with those agencies how successful their use of advertising has been historically and how it would be for your brand. It is important to acquire additional knowledge about other areas of marketing, such as what particular trade shows the prospective licensee attends. Their answers will serve as evidence that the prospective licensee is investing in the same type of marketing that you are investing in and could potentially provide you with an opportunity to align your presence at these trade shows. This can be beneficial in a number of ways. First, it could give you a bigger footprint at the tradeshow. If you have two or three licensees that attend the same trade shows as your brand, you will have the chance to be presented in eight or nine categories thereby widening your presence. Second, the cooperation between your company and the licensees will be recognized in the marketplace. Third, it shows that the licensees are investing in the same areas as you, which means there is alignment.

Another area of importance includes how strongly the prospective licensee will stand behind their product, so be sure to include questions such as: "What kind of product guarantees and warranties do you offer?" Their answer will enable you to determine whether they are at the level of your product guarantees and warranties or are they even better? If the prospective licensee's product guarantees or warranties are worse than yours that is a concern and you should be aware of it.

B. ___If your company uses an advertising agency, specify:

| Key Contact | |
| --- | --- |
| Firm Name | |
| Address | |
| Phone | |

C. Which trade shows does the company currently display?

D. Product guarantees/warranties: Describe your current guarantee and/or warranty programs.

Understanding the **Manufacturing** process that the licensee takes to manufacture a product is an important aspect to know and this is why it is included in the Licensee Application. Specific questions that you should ask the prospective licensees are: "Where do you manufacture your product? Is it manufactured abroad or is it done domestically? What kind of standards do you have? How do you audit those manufacturing facilities? Are the facilities company owned or are they third-party manufacturers? Will you be manufacturing the product for this license or will you be choosing a third-party manufacturer?" While a prospective licensee may own their own manufacturing facility, or typically use a third-party manufacturing, they may decide to do something different with your particular license. Therefore, it is imperative that you understand the prospective licensee's thought process in how they will be manufacturing the product. You may find out that they actually manufacture in the same third- party facilities that you do. If so, that could give you stronger buyer power with the manufacturer. If you're manufacturing in one facility and you have a large amount, e.g., fifty million dollars of merchandise being manufactured in that facility, and you sign two or three licensees with equivalent amount of production, that is going to give you twice the purchasing volume and "buyer power' with that particular manufacturer. This is an example of an intangible (tertiary) benefit that was referenced in Chapter 1.

## VI. Manufacturing

A. Where does the company manufacture / source its products? Indicate company owned manufacturing facilities and location.

B. Will your company manufacture product for this license?

C. Where will you manufacture the products?

A licensee may choose to use a third-party manufacturer. In this case, the licensee will need to provide you with the third-party manufacturer's contact information so that you can follow up and ask questions about their standards and procedures. In addition, the prospective licensee or their manufacturer will need to provide you with the location of the distribution centers intended to be used. It may be in your best interest to visit the distribution centers provided on the application and assess them. When visiting these centers ask yourself: "Are they well lit? Are they well maintained? Do they use technology or do they use manual labor, or a combination of both?"

D. If using a third party manufacturer, list details:

| | |
|---|---|
| Name | |
| Address | |
| Contact | |
| Phone | |
| Email | |

E. What steps/process does the company use in its quality control procedures?

F. Location of Distribution/Shipping Points?

Let's look at some more information as it relates to the **Proposed Licensing Information.** You have taken intense measures and used a large number of resources to ensure that your brand is perceived the way you want. So, having a clear understanding of how the prospective licensee plans to use your brand is critical. For instance, if your brand represents living a healthy lifestyle, but the licensee is planning to use your brand to promote food that is made with less than the highest quality ingredients, it is absolutely necessary to know this beforehand. You need to know what products the prospective licensee intends to make with your brand. Without this understanding, your prospect could develop a product that does not align with your Brand Expansion Point, which can ultimately cause damage to the brand. Also, require the prospective licensee to explain the kind of market size they are considering for your particular category. As the prospective licensee completes the product licensing information, there are seven different questions they need to answer accurately. (1) What is the size of the total market for the proposed product(s)? (2) What percent of the company sales do these products under different names currently represent? (3) Who are the primary competitors in the space, in the category that they want to license your brand? For example, when I ran the Rubbermaid licensing program we were looking at one point to extend the brand into the trash bag category, in the consumer space. We wanted to find a best-in-class manufacturer who wanted to license our brand. There were big competitors out there such as Glad and Hefty, which our brand would be up against. Before getting too far into the process, we inquired as to how strong our third-party manufacturer was and if they had the resources to compete competitively and successfully in the marketplace with the big brands. That's the kind of information you will be looking for in the Prospective Licensee Application, which we have addressed in this section.

## VII. Proposed License Information

A. For what specific products is the company seeking a license?

B. Brand(s) proposing to License:

| ☐ [Insert Name of Brand] | ☐ [Insert Name of Brand] | ☐ [Insert Name of Brand] |
|---|---|---|
| ☐ [Insert Name of Brand] | ☐ [Insert Name of Brand] | ☐ [Insert Name of Brand] |
| ☐ [Insert Name of Brand] | ☐ [Insert Name of Brand] | ☐ [Insert Name of Brand] |

C. Describe the current retail and market conditions for the proposed products:

D. Market Size

1. Size of total market for the proposed product(s). List separately if the products represent different product categories (e.g., home furnishings vs. automobiles vs. apparel.)

| Product Category | $ |
|---|---|
|  | $ |
|  | $ |
|  | $ |

2. What percent of the company's sales do these products under different names currently represent?

| Product | % |
|---|---|
|  | % |
|  | % |
|  | % |
|  | % |
|  | % |

3. Who are the primary competitors for the proposed products, and what is their estimated share of the market?

| Competitor | Share |
|---|---|
| | % |
| | % |
| | % |
| | % |
| | % |

(4) How will the proposed products look and differ from the competition and in which way will you be similar? Certain features represent "points of parity" and are standard in the marketplace. The features your prospective licensee can offer to differentiate your brand are going to be the key drivers of success. (5) What is the pricing that they are proposing for your product at wholesale and what is the suggested retail price? The question addresses how a prospective licensee's pricing structure correlates with your own pricing structure and to your competitors in the marketplace. (6) What are the Projected Annual Sales of the proposed product? Here is the first time your prospective licensee will share their thinking on what the Projected Annual Sales of that proposed branded product are going to look like for Year 1 and Year 2. This will give you a snapshot of how much the prospective licensees are willing to invest in your brand in this category. This forecast should be one of the first areas you want to look at to see whether or not they even are in the ballpark from where you want the brand to be regarding sales and market share. If your brand is at 15 percent, 20 percent or 30 percent market share in all your other categories, then you have a good expectation of where the brand should be long term. These are the percentages you should be anticipating your licensee to reach in an extended category over time.

4. How will the proposed products differ from the competition and your company's other, similar products? (For example, features, technology, design, function, color, graphics, etc.)

5. Proposed pricing (Attach Additional Pages if Necessary):

| Product | Wholesale | Retail |
|---------|-----------|--------|
|  |  |  |
|  |  |  |
|  |  |  |
|  |  |  |
|  |  |  |

6. Projected annual sales of proposed product (by items):

| Product | Year 1 | Year 2 |
|---------|--------|--------|
|  |  |  |
|  |  |  |
|  |  |  |
|  |  |  |
|  |  |  |

(7) How is your third-party manufacturer, your prospective licensee, going to achieve that for you? For this question, you are asking the licensees to here to rank the channel where they have the greatest strength. Once completed you are going to look at these channels and mirror them up against where you are today and where you desire to stand. If the prospective licensee is in channels where you are today, but they are also in channels where you want to be, then this is going to be a great opportunity for you to extend into those channels.

Why does this matter? Well first, it's going to connect you with consumers in channels you currently aren't in today. Second, the licensees are going to start establishing relationships with your brand in your chosen channel, which is going to allow you to have a relationship with that particular retailer. You may even have the opportunity to bring all of your core products into that channel. This is a compelling benefit that comes from licensing your brand to a strong licensee. If your core products are suitable for that channel, this is a tremendous way for you to get those core products in that channel and drive tremendous growth for your company.

7. Rank the Channel for selling these products.
   1 –10, with 1 as the strongest channel, and 10 as the weakest

| | |
|---|---|
| Airlines | Kiosks |
| Amusement Parks | Mass Markets |
| Art / Craft Stores | Mid Tier |
| Book Stores | Music Retailers |
| Cash & Carry | Newsstands |
| Catalog Sales | Retail Stores |
| Convenience Stores | Schools |
| Chain Stores | Specialist Multiples |
| Department Stores | Speciality Stores |
| Direct Mail | Sporting Goods Stores |
| Direct Sales | Stationary stores |
| Duty Free | Toy Stores |
| Event / Value / Arena | TV Home Shopping |
| Food & Drug | Vending Distribution |
| Fundraiser | Warehouses |
| Gift Stores | Whole Stores |
| Hobby / Model Stores | Others: |
| Home / Hardware Stores | |
| Home Video Rental | |
| Houseware Stores | |
| Hypermarkets | |

| Independent Retailers | | |
|---|---|---|
| Internet | | |

In the **Proposed Licensing Terms** section, the product categories are defined along with the length of the term. A minimum three years is suggested for the term, but the license could last five years or longer. The reason why you want to sign a minimum three-year license is because it could take up to two years to commercialize a product. In this case you would have one or two years after the commercialization date to evaluate whether or not to renew the license. This way you get a return on your investment, and the licensee gets a return on their investment as well. Naturally, the licensee is going to invest more if you give them a longer period of time. Finally, let's look at the marketing dates for the trade launch and first shipment. The prospective licensee should be asked: "When do you think you're going to launch the product in the trade? When do you think you are going to make their first shipment? When do you think you are going to commercialize our brand in the category that you're asking to license?"

## VIII. Proposed License Terms

Product Category:

A. Territory(ies) proposing to sell products:

| □ United States | □ Africa | □ Australia |
|---|---|---|
| □ Brazil | □ Canada | □ China |
| □ France | □ Germany | □ Ireland |
| □ Israel | □ Japan | □ Korea |
| □ Mexico | □ New Zealnd | □ Singapore |
| □ Spain | □ Taiwan | □ United Kingdom |
| **Specify Others** | □ Other Asia | □ Other Europe |
| | □ Other Latin America | □ Other |

B. Length of license term (number of years): _____

C. Marketing Dates (Month/Year):

  a. Trade Lunch: _____

  b. First Shipment: _____

Next you want to understand where the prospective license will be in retail and in wholesale dollar volume under a low assumption, medium assumption, and a high assumption. This will give you a conservative understanding of where they're going to be, a realistic scenario and a best-case scenario. If everything goes as planned, you will have an understanding at the top end; however if everything doesn't go as planned, you will know the bottom end. Similarly, with the rest of these particular areas, you'll know the wholesale dollar volume, the average wholesale price per unit, the units sold, and the number of doors, i.e. stores for each retailer. This is great information to help you understand what the prospective licensee thinks it can do with your brand in the category they are asking to license. You want to determine if their objectives are feasible. The prospective licensee will need to complete this forecast, which is an extensive exercise. Moreover they will want to complete the application to earn your business and the right to use your brand in a particular category.

D. Sales Projections (list separately by proposed country if applicable):

| Three Year Sales Projections | Low Assumption | Medium Assumption | High Assumption |
|---|---|---|---|
| YEAR 1 | | | |
| Retail Dollar Value | | | |
| Wholesale Dollar Volume | | | |
| Avg. Retail Price Per Unit | | | |
| Avg Wholesale Price Per Unit | | | |

That concludes our chapter on the Licensing Application. We look forward to reviewing The Conservative Business Estimator in the next chapter.

# Chapter 9

# Define Licensing Opportunity 2

In Part I of "Define Licensing Opportunity," the chapter guided you on how to create an application that encompassed every component that you would need to know about your prospective licensees. However, there is much more to learn as you move into Part II. Yes, the application may be completed at this point, but once you have decided on your preferred licensee, certain protocols must take place to solidify the do's and the don'ts for both parties. In Part II you will use information from the Licensee Application and The Conservative Business Estimator, which will be discussed in this chapter, to determine Deal Terms that will lead to a drafted contract.

It is time for you to become familiar with The Conservative Business Estimator which is a forecasting tool that you'll ask the prospective licensee to use. After the "Due Diligence" phase has been completed, you are going to ask the prospective licensees to complete The Conservative Business Estimator form. This consists of the prospects providing a three-year detailed forecast by region, channel, retailer, SKUs, and annual product innovation. This vitality is critical to the long-term success of their program and your brand in that particular category. The sales projections and viability are then compared across all the licensee candidates to see which is going to get chosen to become the licensee in that category. Never have just one option; you should always have at least two or three candidates from which to choose. Why? You may have a prospective licensee that is best-in-class with the most revenue, resources and market share, but only wants to invest a small amount against your program. On the other hand you may have a smaller licensee, who will make a considerable investment. The one who makes the larger investment is going to be a better choice for you if everything else is equal. So, let's dive into how to complete The Conservative Business Estimator.

Below is a representation of The **Conservative Business Estimator** (Figure 9-1). In continuation from section to section, the red highlighted blocked

<u>areas are the ones to maintain your focus.</u> As you can see in this section the estimator is asking for the type of product to be listed by **Stock Keeping Unit** (SKU). Suppose that the product is a kitchen stepladder that provides one, two, and three-step stepladders. If there were more than one SKU the licensee would list that as well.

## The Conservative Business Estimator

**PRODUCT BY SKU**

| | (Enter Retailer Name) | | | |
|---|---|---|---|---|
| | **% of Total Business** | | **100%** | |
| | **Est. # Doors** | **Est. $/Door** | **Est. Units/Door** | |
| | 2000 | $184 | 59 | |
| **Licensed Products** | **Est. Unit Price** | **Est. Unit Sold** | **Est. Wholesale Sales** | **Projected % of Business $** |
| **Example Product** | $3.14 | 117,000 | $367,380 | 100.0% |
| | $0.00 | | $0 | 0.0% |
| | $0.00 | | $0 | 0.0% |
| | $0.00 | | $0 | 0.0% |
| *Wholesale Totals* | | 117,000 | $367,380 | 100.0% |

*Figure 9-1 The Conservative Business Estimator: SKU*

Take a look at the **Estimated Unit Price** (Figure 9-2). This is the price at which the branded stepladder is going to be sold to the retailer and also the wholesale price from which royalties would be calculated.

**WHOLESALE PRICE** at which licensee sells licensed product to their retailer.

| | (Enter Retailer Name) | | | |
|---|---|---|---|---|
| | **% of Total Business** | | **100%** | |
| | **Est. # Doors** | **Est. $/Door** | **Est. Units/Door** | |
| | 2000 | $184 | 59 | |
| ...d Products | **Est. Unit Price** | **Est. Unit Sold** | **Est. Wholesale Sales** | **Projected % of Business $** |
| **Example Product** | $3.14 | 117,000 | $367,380 | 100.0% |
| | $0.00 | | $0 | 0.0% |
| | $0.00 | | $0 | 0.0% |
| | $0.00 | | $0 | 0.0% |
| *Wholesale Totals* | | 117,000 | $367,380 | 100.0% |

*Figure 9-2 Wholesale Price*

Next, have the prospective licensee calculate the **Estimated Units Sold** (Figure 9-3); how many units they estimate they are going to sell to that particular retailer. The **Estimated Unit Price** is $3.14 and the Estimated Units Sold are 117,000. That number by itself conveys an understanding that the prospective licensee's thought process is thorough. How should you be able tell? It is not a round number like a 100,000 or 200,000. The licensee came up with an exact unit, which reveals they took the time to perform an ample amount of research to come to that conclusion.

*ESTIMATED UNITS of licensed product the licensee is expected to sell.*

| | (Enter Retailer Name) | | | |
|---|---|---|---|---|
| | **% of Total Business** | | **100%** | |
| | **Est. # Doors** | **Est. $/Door** | **Est. Units/Door** | |
| | 2000 | $184 | 59 | |
| **Licensed Products** | **Est. Unit Price** | **Est. Unit Sold** | **Est. Wholesale Sales** | **Projected % of Business $** |
| **Example Product** | $3.14 | 117,000 | $367,380 | 100.0% |
| | $0.00 | | $0 | 0.0% |
| | $0.00 | | $0 | 0.0% |
| | $0.00 | | $0 | 0.0% |
| *Wholesale Totals* | | 117,000 | $367,380 | 100.0% |

*Figure 9-3 Estimated Units Sold*

Now focus your attention on the **Estimated Wholesales Sales** number (Figure 9-4). This is simply the calculation of the Estimated Unit Price times the number of Units Sold. In this particular case, you would take the Estimated Unit Price and multiply it by the Estimated Units Sold to arrive at the total Estimated Wholesales Sales number.

| | (Enter Retailer Name) | | | |
|---|---|---|---|---|
| | **% of Total Business** | | **100%** | |
| | **Est. # Doors** | **Est. $/Door** | **Est. Units/Door** | |
| | 2000 | $184 | 59 | |
| **Licensed Products** | **Est. Unit Price** | **Est. Unit Sold** | **Est. Wholesale Sales** | **Projected % of** |
| **Example Product** | $3.14 | 117,000 | $367,380 | |
| | $0.00 | | $0 | |
| | $0.00 | | $0 | |
| | $0.00 | | $0 | |
| *Wholesale Totals* | | 117,000 | $367,380 | |

*ESTIMATED WHOLESALE DOLLAR SALES = Estimated Unit Price x Estimated Units Sold*

*Figure 9-4 Estimated Wholesales Sales*

*Estimated Unit Price × Estimated Unit Sold= Estimated Wholesales Sales*

*(3.14 x 117,000 = 367,380)*

After the Wholesales Sales number has been computed, the **Projected Percentage of Business** (Figure 9-5) is determined. If you have one SKU, the projected percentage will be 100 percent. If you have two SKUs, they should combine to equal 100 percent. Here is how you calculate the projected percentage of the business:

| | (Enter Retailer Name) | | | |
|---|---|---|---|---|
| | **% of Total Business** | | **100%** | |
| | **Est. # Doors** | **Est. $/Door** | **Est. Units/Door** | |
| | 2000 | $184 | 59 | |
| **Licensed Products** | **Est. Unit Price** | **Est. Unit Sold** | **Est. Wholesale Sales** | **Projected % of Business $** |
| **Example Product** | $3.14 | 117,000 | $367,380 | 100.0% |
| | $0.00 | | $0 | 0.0% |
| | $0.00 | | $0 | |
| | $0.00 | | $0 | |
| **Wholesale Totals** | | 117,000 | $367,380 | |

*Figure 9-5 Projected Percentage of Business Dollars*

*PROJECTED % OF BUSINESS $*
= Estimated Wholesale Sales / Total Estimated Wholesale Sales

*(Estimated Wholesale Sales) / (Total Estimated Wholesale Sale)*
*= Projected Percentage of Business*

In this case, there is only have one example so, it's a 100 percent of the total.

The **Percentage of Total Business** by the **Number of Doors** (Figure 9-6) is also computed in The Conservative Business Estimator. The term "Number of Doors" is nomenclature that is used in the industry to reference the number of retail stores for a particular channel or specifically for a particular retailer. Assume in this case that Walmart has 6,000 stores globally. However, since a licensed product is for a particular category and only specific retail stores of a large retailer may be appropriate to sell your branded product, the likelihood is that only a portion of the total "doors" will get the brand product. The prospective licensee might forecast 2,000 of Walmart's total 6,000 retail stores will take the product.

| | (Enter Retailer Name) | | | |
|---|---|---|---|---|
| | **% of Total Business** | | **100%** | |
| | **Est. # Doors** | **Est. $/Door** | **Est. Units/Door** | |
| | 2000 | =367380/2000 | 59 | |
| **Licensed Products** | **Est. Unit Price** | **Est. Unit Sold** | **Est. Wholesale Sales** | **Projected % of Business $** |
| **Example Product** | $3.14 | 117,000 | $367,380 | 100.0% |
| | $0.00 | | $0 | 0.0% |
| | $0.00 | | $0 | 0.0% |
| | $0.00 | | $0 | 0.0% |
| **Wholesale Totals** | | 117,000 | $367,380 | 100.0% |

*Figure 9-6 Percentage of Total Business by the Number of Doors*

Next the **Estimated Units Sold** and is divided by the **Estimated Number of Doors** to generate a **Unit Per Door** value (Figure 9-7).

| | (Enter Retailer Name) | | | |
|---|---|---|---|---|
| | **% of Total Business** | | **100%** | |
| | **Est. # Doors** | **Est. $/Door** | **Est. Units/Door** | |
| | 2000 | $184 | =117000/2000 | |
| **Licensed Products** | **Est. Unit Price** | **Est. Unit Sold** | **Est. Wholesale Sales** | **Projected % of Business $** |
| **Example Product** | $3.14 | 117,000 | $367,380 | 100.0% |
| | $0.00 | | $0 | 0.0% |
| | $0.00 | | $0 | 0.0% |
| | $0.00 | | $0 | 0.0% |
| **Wholesale Totals** | | 117,000 | $367,380 | 100.0% |

*Figure 9-7 Estimated Units Sold Divided by Estimated Number of Doors*

**(Estimated Units Sold) 117,000÷(Estimated Number of Doors)2000**

A completed estimator will help you understand, in detail, the size of the opportunity as it relates to licensing your brand in the particular category.

Since you have learned about The Conservative Business Estimator and how to use it for your selection purposes, let's get a better understanding of how common Deal terms are used. To begin, you will start with the information provided by the Licensee Application and The Conservative Business Estimator. This information will aid you in determining the specific Deal Terms you want to place in the contract. By creating the Deal Terms this way, the prospective licensees will likely support what you are asking for since it is based on the information that they have provided you. This offers an opportunity for the program to be successful and for both you and the manufacturer to be aligned. Ultimately these Deal Terms will form the basis for the licensing agreement, which is the legal document that governs a relationship that the two of you have.

***

Deal terms include:

**Trademarks** – these should be specified in the agreement. Annotated are the trademarks that the licensee is allowed to use in conjunction with the covered products. Being clear here is especially important if the manufacturer is licensing from a company that owns multiple trademarks. As an illustration, suppose an apparel licensee wants a license from Disney. Since Disney has access to hundreds of trademarks, they would list on this Deal Term Sheet which particular trademarks they will allow the licensee to use. Disney could grant the licensee permission to use Winnie the Pooh, Mickey Mouse, and the Seven Dwarfs or they might grant permission to license other characters such as Doc McStuffins, Cinderella, or Little Einsteins. It just depends on what Disney is comfortable with, what the licensee wants, and what makes the most sense at the time.

**Cover Products** – this is the category to be created. It should specify in the agreement what products will be sold by the licensee that bear the trademark of the licensor. In other words, the definition of the category specific to the license should be written here.

**Authorized Channels** - these are the channels that the licensee wants to sell your brand in the category that they've selected. The channels listed need to align with the channels that you want the licensed product sold.

**Territory** - these are the region(s) or country(s) identified in the agreement. The territory that the licensee wants to sell your product in should align with where your core branded products are currently sold, the trademark is registered, and the brand has high awareness.

**Term** - this is the period, typically in years, in which the agreement shall be in effect with a beginning and ending date. You might have a specific timeframe in mind that is different from the specific timeframe in mind that the licensee has in mind. It is vital that both parties agree on these timeframes.

**Exclusivity** - this term ensures whether or not the manufacturer will be the only licensee for the licensor's brands in the category of Covered Products specified in the agreement. This means that the manufacturer knows that your trademark or your brand is going to be given only to them in the particular category. No other companies are going to have the right to sell merchandise with your brand on it in the category that you are asking it to be sold. Normally companies do not offer Exclusivity because it limits the brand owner's ability to choose another licensee if the first one does not meet the expectations of the agreement. If you choose to agree to Exclusivity your hands are tied even if the licensee fails to meet expectations. This puts them in a position of weakness.

**Royalty Rate** - this is probably the most crucial term in the agreement because the Royalty Rate determines the amount of royalties that have to be paid by the manufacturer to the licensor. The Royalty Rates set a benchmark for the brand. A great brand like one owned by Disney can demand 12 percent-14 percent Royalty Rate, or even higher. That's a significant percentage of the Net Sales. Conversely, an up and coming brand might only demand 5 percent or 6 percent. Then there are some hot market brands, e.g. the current World Series Champions, which for a specified period of time may command a Royalty Rate as much as 20 percent.

**Advance** – this is cash paid upon signature of the licensing agreement. This provision puts teeth in the agreement as the licensee has to make an investment in the license before they've sold one unit of product. That tells the licensor that the licensee is going to do everything in her power to stay focused on that agreement in order to reclaim the money paid out and make the program bigger. Typically, an Advance is to equal 50 percent of the first-year minimum guaranteed royalties.

**Minimum Guarantees** – these are Guaranteed Quarterly Royalty Payments that a company has to pay to a brand owner over a year. Typically, the Minimum Guarantee is 25 percent to 40 percent of the projected royalty that should be derived by the agreement. For example, where Year 1 the projected royalty is a 100, Year 2 is 300, and Year 3 is 500. If the projected Minimum Guaranty were 25 percent of that total, it would be 25 for Year 1, 75 for Year 2, and 125 for Year 3.

**New Product Innovations** – these are often required by the licensor on an annual basis to ensure that the licensee is sufficiently investing R&D into the agreement and that the Covered Products sold maintain relevance and desirability. New product innovation is critical to the strength and the success of any program. The Conservative Business Estimator helps in understanding why the licensee is arriving at their forecast. As the brand owner, you might have a minimum requirement of new product innovations for particular category. This is something that should not be overlooked.

**Sales Performance Requirements** – these are similar to Minimum Guarantees, but instead they are the Minimum Sales the licensee must achieve each year of the licensing agreement. Effectively what you are saying to the manufacturer is that it is not good enough to pay a Minimum Guaranteed Royalty Payment to maintain the license. You want to know that the licensee is actually selling the licensed product to retailers who are commercializing it in the marketplace. It is important for your brand to engage with the consumer in each category in each authorized channel in region. The sales performance requirement is a commitment to this. If a licensee has to pay $100 in Minimum Guarantees per year, then you are expecting to receive 2 – 4 times that amount. Therefore, you want the equivalent amount of sales that would generate $200 – $400 in royalties. Therefore, the expected sales based on a 10 percent Royalty Rate would be ten times the expected royalties. This calculates to be $2000 – $4000 in wholesale sales or $4,000 – $8,000 in retail sales. If each product were to sell for $10, then you would expect 400 – 800 units of branded product to reach consumers on an annual basis. This "consumer engagement" is priceless.

**Shipping Date** – this is the date by which the licensee must first ship licensed products to the retailers to meet their "sale by" date. The licensees should immediately discuss when they expect to have the product shipped and ready to be sold in the marketplace. This information discloses what kind of timeline they are thinking about. That date is important as it tell you when your product is expected to be commercialized. However, it's equally important to make sure that the licensee is set up for success. If the licensee gives you a date that is in your opinion too soon and you know this based on your approval process and timeline, then you need to set them up for success by pushing that date out a sufficient amount for them to meet the Shipping Date.

**Commercialization Date** – this is the date by which the licensee must have placement of their licensed product in each of the Authorized Channels in their contract. The Commercialization Date lets you know when the licensed product is expected to be on the retailers' shelves to connect with the consumer.

***

Prospective licensees are asked to present the overall business plan assuming they hold the license. Once the Licensee Application and The Conservative

Business Estimator are complete, you want the licensees to take all the information that they have compiled up to this point and propose a business plan that assumes that they have received the license. You want them to present the concepts in the channels and in the regions that they requested be stipulated in the license. You want them to tell you why they should earn your business and convince you that this is something that is important to you. Treat this concept review like you are the general manager for this particular category with this particular licensee. When the licensee is presenting the business plan, you want them to treat this presentation as if they currently have your brand in their marketplace in that category. The licensee should explain what are they going to do with the license, i.e. where, when, what price, what SKUs, etc.

# Rubbermaid Case Study

## Overview

The Brand Promise of the Rubbermaid brand is to be the trusted authority for storage and organization solutions. When Rubbermaid signs a license they will provide the licensee with a style guide that includes the logo, visual elements including The Red Wave, and any other core components of the Rubbermaid brand guidelines. The Brand Architecture of the Rubbermaid is broken down into the following elements: (1). The brand's core values, which are enduring, innovation and leadership-forward. (2). The product attributes, which include ergonomic, engineered excellence, ease of use, simplicity and enduring style. (3). The Functional Benefits of the brand include durability, ingeniousness, high quality, essential, and of great value. (4). The Core Message that should be delivered with every product is: Rubbermaid shapes your space so that you can have control and ease of mind with their products. (5). The Emotional Benefits of the Rubbermaid brand include creativity, customizable, control, respect and trust and overall fun. (6). The Brand Essence or Promise is Rubbermaid helps empower me.

# Brand Architecture

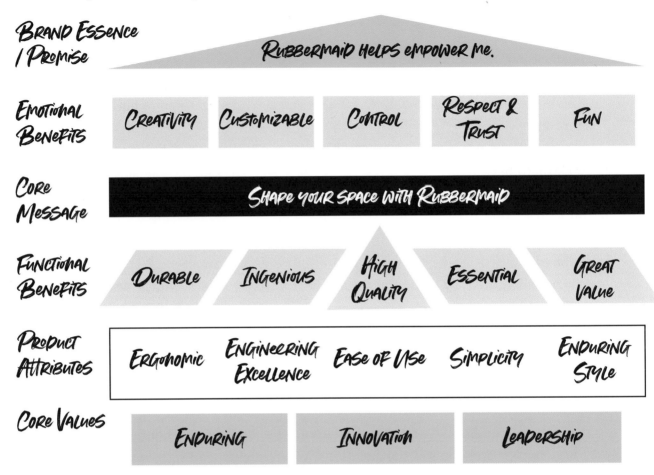

**Brand Essence / Promise**
Rubbermaid helps empower me.

**Emotional Benefits**
Creativity | Customizable | Control | Respect & Trust | Fun

**Core Message**
Shape your space with Rubbermaid

**Functional Benefits**
Durable | Ingenious | High Quality | Essential | Great Value

**Product Attributes**
Ergonomic | Engineering Excellence | Ease of Use | Simplicity | Enduring Style

**Core Values**
Enduring | Innovation | Leadership

*Figure 9-8 Rubbermaid Brand Architecture*

## Background:

- There are two candidate licensees
- The category is "home ladders"
- The brand is Rubbermaid
- The brand owner is asking each licensee candidate to assume that the overall home ladder size for the North America market is $300M.

## Objective:

Choose the best licensee who is capable of the following:

- Creating a product that reinforces the Rubbermaid brand position
- Selling into the Home Improvement, Mass and Department Store channels

- Distributing products in the US and Canada
- Achieving at least 10 percent market share in 3 years

## Target:
Self-assured balancers: independent, proactive women ages 18-54 who, in seeking to balance their lives (family, work, relationships, and self), put so much into their day that they need to replenish what's been taken out.

## Frame of Reference:
Rubbermaid is a 100 year-old American icon (serving consumer and commercial users primarily in organization, storage, and cleaning products)

## Point of Difference:
Provides ingeniously durable ways to personalize your environment, so you feel empowered

## Support:
Because Rubbermaid uses high-quality materials to ensure long lasting product designed to get the job done easily and quickly every time. By blending technical innovation with beautiful colors, artistic lines and excellent craftsmanship. Rubbermaid offers products that fit your individual taste.

## Case:
Here are the prototypes of Licensee A and Licensee B.

**Licensee A**　　　　　**Licensee B**

Licensee A has a three steps stepladder with a tube structure. Overall it looks stable and appears to have long lasting durability. The Rubbermaid logo is on the top of the ladder. Licensee B has a rectangular shape structure and has the red wave element is embedded in each of the three steps with the Rubbermaid brand embedded in them. It also includes a shelf that provides space on top the provides the customer who purchases the items an added benefit of carrying any tools or additional items needing to be temporarily stored for the project at hand. The Rubbermaid logo is on the top shelf, the top of the ladder, and the steps.

Licensee A has built relationship with channels that are selling in Walmart, Target, Kmart, JC Penny, Sears. Their yearly subtotals, in millions, are $22, $31 and $42 and that is in the US market. In channels in Canada they are selling in Canadian Tire, RONA, and Walmart with subtotals, in millions, of $3, $6 and $9 for total sales in Year 1 of $25, $37 and $51. For licensee B, they have built relationships with channels that are selling in the US in Sears, Target, Home Depot and JC Penny with subtotals, in millions, of $18, $28 and $35. In addition, they sell in Canada with Canadian Tire, The Bay, and Walmart with subtotals, in millions, of $3, $5 and $9. Licensee B sales overall are $21, $33 and $44. Both are relatively comparable in retail channels and total sales.

|  | Year 1 | Year 2 | Year 3 |  | Year 1 | Year 2 | Year 3 |
| --- | --- | --- | --- | --- | --- | --- | --- |
| **USA** |  |  |  | **USA** |  |  |  |
| Walmart | $10 | $12 | $15 | Sears | $7 | $8 | $9 |
| Target | $5 | $8 | $10 | Target | $8 | $11 | $13 |
| Kmart | $3 | $5 | $7 | Home Depot | $1 | $2 | $3 |
| JC Penny | $2 | $3 | $5 | JC Penny | $2 | $7 | $10 |
| Sears | $2 | $3 | $5 | **Subtotal** | $18 | $28 | $35 |
| **Subtotal** | $22 | $31 | $42 | **Canada** |  |  |  |
| **Canada** |  |  |  | Canadian Tire | $1 | $2 | $3 |
| Canadian Tire | $2 | $3 | $4 | The Bay | $1 | $2 | $4 |
| RONA | $1 | $2 | $3 | Walmart | $1 | $1 | $2 |
| Walmart | $0 | $1 | $2 | **Subtotal** | $3 | $5 | $9 |
| **Subtotal** | $3 | $6 | $9 | **Total** | $21 | $33 | $44 |
| **Total** | $25 | $37 | $51 |  |  |  |  |

*Figure 9-9 Rubbermaid Financial Projections In Millions*

**Take A Glance:**

Looking back at the objective criteria given above, identify which respective channels are part of the agreement. Did you find Home Improvement, Mass, and Department Store channels that are able to achieve a 10 percent share in three years? If so, you are correct.

Licensee A is in Mass but does not have presence in the Home Improvement channels except for Rona, which is in Canada. Licensee B is in Mass with Target, Home Improvement with Home Depot, and Department Stores with Sears. Similarly, they are also in Canadian Tire, Walmart, and The Bay. From here it is easy to determine that Licensee B meets all the criteria, but Licensee A does not.

Who should be chosen and why? Refer back to Figure 9-3. Licensee B has embedded the brand attributes into the ladder that they've chosen. For instance, they've built the red wave into the padding on the footsteps; they've put the logo on the product, and they've placed a tray on near the top of the ladder for easy storage and functionality, which fulfills their brand promise. Plus, if the Rubbermaid logo is removed from the top, the consumer would still be able to determine that the product is a Rubbermaid branded product. Licensee A, this looks more like a standard three steps stepladder with limited differentiation. From the brand owner's perspective Licensee B is a preferred choice.

Additionally, the channels for Licensee A did not involve retailers in the home improvement channel in the US nor did they project 10 percent market share by Year 3 and thus, did not meeting the specified criteria. It could be inferred there was $300M in total sales for this particular channel thus enabling both Licensee A and Licensee B to reach their goal of $30M in sales (10 percent market share).

**Results:**

The best choice, based on the criteria presented from this case study, would be Licensee B. Did you choose the same licensee?

\*\*\*

After deciding which licensee has the best licensing opportunity, you will need to finalize the terms and other elements to develop the basis for the contract; this information should give you that criteria. Then you want to confer with the category manager and brand team to make sure that everybody is aligned on why the particular licensee meets the standards, criteria, and performance ratings that are needed to be successful. Finally review the goals with each department and with senior management to ensure they are aware, committed, and accountable. As a licensing manager, you don't want to do this deal by yourself; you want to get buy-in by everyone in the department to make sure they are behind you. Similarly, you want the same kind of level of buy-in by the licensee.

In summary, when determining the Deal Terms, the licensing team, or the agent you will use the information from the Licensee Application and The Conservative Business Estimator to create the Deal Term Summary. Then you will review the product concepts through the presentation to help evaluate which company is the best choice. Pay close attention to the concepts, the estimated sales targets, and whether they've embedded the criteria of the brand in the product. Once completed, confer with the marketing department, the product development team, the legal department, and operations to get everyone's buy-in and support. Now that you have all the information needed you are ready to have the contract drafted. Work with the legal team to complete the draft contract then send to the licensee for their review.

Congratulations, you've completed this step of the process!

# Chapter 10

# Negotiating Contract - Part 1

Negotiating a contract can often be overwhelming for you especially when trying to license your product to a manufacturer. This is especially true since every organization has different needs and goals to fulfill through the process. Since the value of the Deal Terms will be unique to every licensing contract, they must be negotiated between you, the licensor and the prospective licensee. In this chapter, you will have an opportunity to learn exactly how to negotiate a contract to create a "win-win" situation for both you and your licensee. To increase your understanding of this topic the chapter has been divided into two separate sections. In this first section, the discussion will focus on Agreeing Deal Terms and how to get the Internal Approval Sheet approved. Let's begin.

As you learned in Chapter 9, the information derived from the Licensee Application and The Conservative Business Estimator is used to create the **Deal Term Summary.** This information was provided by the prospective licensee and essentially is what they believe is achievable through the license. These beliefs should be taken into consideration in defining the Deal Terms; this ensures a viable agreement is created that both parties can accept.

Looking at the Deal Term Summary below, the specific things you want to know are to complete it are: Who is the prospective licensee? What is their address? What is the Scope of License? This includes the Trademarks, Covered Products, Authorized Channels, the Territory, the Term including the Initial Term, and the Extended Term (only upon mutual agreement of the parties). The Insurance requirements for each occurrence and in aggregate should also be included in the Deal Term Summary.

# Deal Term Summary

This deal term summary sets forth certain for a proposed license agreement between the parties. The parties agree that this summary is not a contract and is not binding on either party.

Proposed Licensee:

Licensee address:

Type of entity and state under which Licensee is formed (e.g. a Delaware corporation):

## Scope of License:

Trademarks:

Covered Products:

Authorized Channels:

Territory:

Term:

    Initial Term:

    Extended Term (only upon mutual agreement of the parties):

Insurance Requirements:

    US$ _____ per occurrence
    US$ _____ aggregate

Required limits may be satisfied by a combination of primary General Products, Umbrella, can/ or Excess Liability Insurance policies.

Now that you have received a little background on the Deal Term Summary, let's take each section and focus on specific details related to that area starting with the prospective licensee. In this section you want to gain an understanding of the kind of company you are dealing with: What type of legal entity are they? What state are they registered? Are they an international company? Then move to the scope of the license. What trademarks do they want to license from you? For example, when I worked at Newell Brands (formerly Newell Rubbermaid) we owned dozens of brands, which we licensed including Calphalon, Graco, Rubbermaid, Sharpe and many others. Next look at the covered products section. In the Rubbermaid case study, the covered products were "step ladders for home use". Next, what are the authorized channels the licensee wants to sell the branded product? Do they want to sell into the mass-market channel, the department store channel, sport specialty channel, boutiques, Internet, or home shopping? How does that channel align with your brand? Then look at the territory. Is this for Italy, Germany, North America, Mexico, United States, or Canada? How does that territory align with your brand and its trademarks? What is the initial term? Is it 3, 4, or 5 years? Does this licensee want an extended period and are you prepared to allow the license an extended period of time? And if so, how long would that be? An extended period is used as a renewal guideline based on the success of the initial term.

Proposed Licensee:

Licensee address:

Type of entity and state under which Licensee is formed (e.g., a Delaware corporation):

### Scope of License

Trademarks:

Covered Products:

Authorized Channels:

Territory:

Term:

    Initial Term:

    Extended Term (only upon mutual agreement of the parties):

The Insurance requirements are important as well. Based on the criteria of the particular category to be licensed, the insurance requirement may differ. For instance, the Graco brand's insurance requirements are significantly higher than many consumer product categories considering they are providing car seats for infants, whereas a basic bathroom mat would require a lower level of insurance.

Another specific aspect of the Deal Terms Summary you want to know is the kind of Royalty and Payment Terms. As previously stated in Chapter 9, top brands require 10 – 12 percent royalty, hot market brands 14 – 20 percent, and up and coming brands 5 percent – 8 percent. So, think about the Royalty Rate that you and the licensee can agree upon. Then consider the Advance the licensee is going to pay you. Remember an Advance is typically 50 percent of the first year's Minimum Guaranteed Royalty. Then set the Guaranteed Minimum Royalties and agree those for the initial and for a potential extended term.

Insurance Requirements:

US$ _____ per occurence
US$ _____ aggregate

Required limits may be satisfied by a combination of primary General Products, Umbrella, and/or Excess Liability Insurance policies

### Royalty and Payment Terms

Royalty Rate:

Advance:

The Advance payment may be offset against Royalties due during the period that ends on December 31, _____.

Guaranteed Minimum Periodic Royalty Payments (by country and by period):

Initial Term:

In the event the parties elect to extend the Term of the Agreement for the Extended Term, the Guaranteed Minimum Periodic Royalty Payments for the Extended Term are:

In the **Marketing and Sales** commitments area, there should be specific performance requirements as it relates to sales. Take time to produce a layout of the sales performance per year for that particular category. Then look at the Shipping Date to see when the product will be shipped after it is manufactured and sold in the marketplace. The Shipping Date leads to the Commercialization Date, which is the expected date that the product will be on the shelf. If the process progresses faster than anticipated, that is okay, but the set Commercialization Date should not be postponed.

## Marketing and Sales

Schedule of Minimum New Product Introduction (per year):

Sales Performance Requirements (per year):

Shipping Date:

The Shipping Date means the date by which the Licensee must first ship Licensed Products to the retailers for sales by the retailers.

Commercialization Date:

The Commercialization Date is the date by which Licensee must have placement by each Licensed Product in no less than two of the top five retailers or other entities in each of the Authorized Channels in each country of the Territory.

***

**Signing the Deal Term Summary** is a vital component of a successful licensing program. In my experiences after all these Deal Terms are negotiated, you will have a verbal understanding of the terms, as will the licensee. By laying out each of the Deal Terms, with the specific language on the Deal Term Summary, the prospective licensee can review it and decide to agree or disagree with what you've said. Hopefully, most of the information is going to capture what has been agreed. If not, the Deal Term Summary will create an opportunity for you to discuss those components that have not been thoroughly fleshed out. Once a resolution has been made, and the licensee agrees to the Deal Terms, a signature is provided to confirm that they agree and are in alignment with you. These Deal Terms can then be transferred into the licensing contract. The physical signing of the Deal Term Summary does not constitute an actual contract but eliminates any confusion going forward.

The **Royalty Rates Ranges** depend on the strength of the brand in the category that's being licensed. Not only should a brand have strength is a category, but it is equally important for that brand also to have profitability in the category. For example, when I oversaw the Coca- Cola Olympic pin program, the Royalty Rate on those pins was 20 percent. The reason it was 20 percent is because that particular category has a higher profit margin than many other categories. This meant that the category could bare a higher Royalty Rate and still provide enough profitability for the licensee in order for the program to be successful. In the case of something like a Rubbermaid trash bags or the trash bags in general, those Royalty Rates tend to be lower because the profit margin in resin bags is very narrow.

*Nagano Olympic Trading Pins*

Another component in the process is the **Negotiation Skills** or experience of the parties. There is typically a range of each term that will be a "win-win" between the manufacturer and the brand owner; however, within that range, the strength of the negotiation skills between one party and the other is going to drive where the final terms get defined. Simply put, whether your Royalty Rate is higher or lower will depend on how strong your negotiation skills are compared to the other. Finally, you will want to determine what is each party's **Best Alternative To A Negotiated Agreement (BATNA)**. If one party has a significant number of BATNAs, they may not agree to a Royalty Rate that you would like them to agree. However, if they have limited choices because they've just lost their other license they are going to most likely accept the Royalty Rate that you are asking. If that rate is too high and they accept it anyway the program likely will fail. If you feel you could use help in this area you may wish to review my negotiations guide, "Tilt the Deal to Your Favor: How to Negotiate with Licensees."

***

The **Internal Approval Sheet** is a document that you, as the brand owner will go through. Start with the Non-Exclusive Brand Licensing Deal Overview section. The first thing you'l see is the Brand Positioning Statement. You must make sure everyone understands the Brand Positioning so that the Deal Terms laid out underneath on the Internal Approval Sheet will align with the Brand Positioning. Recall the Brand Positioning is critical to the success of the licensing program. Next, identify the prime mover; this is the internal key person responsible from the brand team for this particular contract. That person's name will go on this Deal Term Summary along with the date. Next, check if this is a new contract, or if it is a renewal contract. In this example, it's a renewal. Then list the prospective licensee, the licensee's address, and the contact name of the person at the licensee's company and their specific information. Lastly, provide the territories the licensee is asking to commercialize with the license. As you can see towards the bottom of this example the renewal is for the countries of Canada and the United States of America.

## NON-EXCLUSIVE BRAND LICENSING DEAL OVERVIEW

**LICENSE/MARKS**  Storage Solutions

**BRAND POSITIONING STATEMENTS**  For adult men who are interested in keeping their personal and at home belongings in one place and well organized. **Storage Solutions** is the brand of organizational products that give you easy and innovative storage because only **Storage Solutions** products are better designed and made than any other brand storage solutions.

**DEAL LEADER/PRIME MOVER**  Pete Canalichio      **DATE:**

**NEW CONTRACT**

**RENEWAL**  X

**PROSPECTIVE LICENSEE**  Excellent Cabinets, Inc.

**PROSPECTIVE LICENSEE ADDRESS:**  123 Cabinet Road
Little Rock, AR

**CONTACT NAME**  John Smith
**TELEPHONE**  888-555-1234
**CELL**  888-555-1235
**FAX**  888-555-1236
**EMAIL**  john.Smith@ExcellentCabinets.com
**WEBSITE**  www.ExcellentCabinets.com

**TERRITORIES**  Canada
United States of America

The next section of the Internal Approval Sheet is the Detailed Description of the contract. This section describes the benefits of the old Deal Terms versus the new. In other words, why should we renew this agreement? In this case you are going from an agreement that had poor cover product definition to one that has a very detailed product definition. It is helpful for both the parties to know the purpose of the license. The next is the product description that specifically informs you on what type of product is important to the prospective licensee. The next area covered is the Royalty Rates. In this example, you have an opportunity for the Royalty Rates to increase over time and to get those Royalty Rates aligned with the brand's inherent value. In the previous agreement, they were set at 5 percent. In this new deal they are going to be set at 7 percent because the brand is strengthening over time and the licensee understands and is willing to pay more of a percentage. In examining the annual revenue stream, you can see that there's an expected increase to $1M in Canada and $5M in the United States. That is the level of detail that is important to be included in the Internal Approval Sheet. When you reference the Product Positioning Statement again you need to be able to understand how, for this particular category, it aligns with the Brand Positioning Statement. This way whatever is created for this specific category will reinforce the Brand Positioning and strengthen the core brand. The NPV (Net Present Value) is also a part of this section. The NPV is defined as sum of the future cash flows, the royalties that are going to be paid over the life of the agreement, discounted at an agreed rate of the return. When an NPV is calculated, the cash in Year 1 (because you are receiving it immediately) has more value than the cash in future years, e.g. Year 3; therefore, you have to discount that cash received proportionately for those future years. The NPV is summation of all those cash flows. Because we don't know what the actual payments will be, the NPV for this Internal Approval Sheet is based on the Minimum Guaranteed Royalties. Then you compare that NPV to the total projected amount of the Minimum Guaranteed Royalties to assess the overall financial value of the deal. In this case, the amount is $2M.

**DETAILED DESCRIPTION OF CONTRACT AGREEMENT:**
(In description include Licensee, Product Description, Length of Contract, Royalty %, Annual Revenue Stream, Termination Fees; in case of a renewal or renegotiation, include benefits of renewal, renegotiation, etc.)

The benefits of this renewal include:

| From: | To: |
| --- | --- |
| Poor Covered Products | Clearly defined Covered Products |
| All channels in US | Mass and Home Improvement |
| Low royalty rates | 1% increase in Year 2 |

Product Description
Ready to Assemble (RTA) wood garage cabinets and shelves, RTS closed shelving, RTA wood furniture, RTA Professional Office Products

Length
6/1/25 to 12/31/28

Royalty Rates
Canada - 5% in 2023 6% in 2024, 7% in 2025

Annual Revenue Stream
Expected revenue will be $1MM in Canada and $5MM in the US in 2025

**PRODUCT POSITIONING STATEMENT(S)**

For adult men who are interested in keeping their basement and garages well organized. Storage Solutions is the brand of cabinets that gives them easy storage because only Storage Solutions products are better designed than other RTA cabinets and are made with durable materials.

**NPV OF CONTRACT (US DOLLARS):** $1.3MM
**INITIAL PAYMENT:** N/A
**TOTAL PROJECT AMOUNT:** $2.0MM

The next part of the Internal Approval Sheet is the Product Launch. In this case, the Trade Launch and the First Shipment are both listed as "ongoing" because this is a contract renewal. Had this been an initial contract you would see a specific date for trade launch and a specific date for the first shipment. However, these do not apply in this particular example. Next is Channels of Distribution, which lists mass retail and home improvement. After the distribution channels are solidified, the Royalty Rate is listed per territory. For the countries of Canada and the United States, we are looking at a 6 percent royalty in Year 1 and a 7 percent royalty in Year 2 in Canada and a 6.5 percent royalty in Year 1 in the United States and a 7 percent royalty in Year 2. The next component addresses the licensee's Annual Marketing Spend. In this instance the licensee agrees to 3 percent of the Net Sales that will be dedicated to marketing the brand in this particular category. An investment in marketing by the licensee is very important for the success of the program and is something that you, as the licensor, should review and something that your internal management will want to see to know that this program has a chance of success. Contributing 3 percent of the overall Net Sales to the overall marketing of the brand will help tremendously.

| PRODUCT LAUNCH: (Quarter, Year) | Trade Launch: | ongoing |
| | First Shipment: | ongoing |

| CHANNELS OF DISTRIBUTION: | Mass Retail Home Improvement |

| ROYALTY RATE: | Canda | |
| | 2024 | 6.0% |
| | 2025 | 7.0% |
| | United States | |
| | 2024 | 6.5% |
| | 2025 | 7.0% |

| LICENSEE'S ANNUAL MARKETING SPEND ($): | Licensee agrees to apply 3% of Net Sales in marketing support to market research and consumer marketing programs. |

Next is the Initial Terms Payment Schedule. These terms will provide how much royalty is going to be guaranteed by year and then how much royalty is going to be guaranteed by payment. Another component here is the Extended Term Notes where both you and the licensor will set additional terms. The Targeted Consumers are also included in this Deal Term Sheet. Understanding the target market is necessary for both parties to know because you don't want the licensee targeting one group while you are targeting another. It is essential to understand where the marketing dollars are to be spent and that each designed product that will be entering the marketplace supports the Brand Positioning.

| INITIAL TERM ANNUAL MINIMUM GUARANTEES: (Payable in Quarterly Installments, Outlined Below) | Year | Guaranteed Minimum $ |
|---|---|---|
| | 2024 (CA) | 200,000 |
| | 2025 (CA) | 250,000 |
| | 2024 (US) | 500,000 |
| | 2025 (US) | 650,000 |

| INITIAL TERM PAYMENT SCHEDULE: Month/Year/Amount Advance is a credit against future earned royalties. Advance is due within 10 business days of contract execution. | | Date Range | | Due Date | Amounts |
|---|---|---|---|---|---|
| | Advance: | | | | |
| | Payment 1: | 01/01/2024 | 03/31/2024 | 03/31/2024 | 175,000 |
| | Payment 2: | 04/01/2024 | 06/31/2024 | 06/31/2024 | 175,000 |
| | Payment 3: | 07/01/2024 | 09/30/2024 | 09/30/2024 | 175,000 |
| | Payment 4: | 10/01/2024 | 12/31/2024 | 12/31/2024 | 175,000 |
| | Payment 5: | 01/01/2025 | 03/31/2025 | 03/31/2025 | 225,000 |
| | Payment 6: | 04/01/2025 | 06/31/2025 | 06/31/2025 | 225,000 |
| | Payment 7: | 07/01/2025 | 09/30/2025 | 09/30/2025 | 225,000 |
| | Payment 8 | 10/01/2025 | 12/31/2025 | 12/31/2025 | 225,000 |

**EXTENDED TERM NOTES:** Renewal Period, Minimums — The companies agree to discuss renewal terms 12 months prior to expiration.

**TARGETED CONSUMERS:** Males 35-54 years old, married, with families.

Special Provisions are yet another component of the Deal Terms Sheet. Any provision that is made should be placed in this section. In our particular case, the discussion focuses on the sales and growth initiative as well as branding. Under the sales and growth initiative the licensee agrees to provide you with monthly updates both orally and in writing during the course of the agreement. Those monthly updates are pertinent to the success of the program. Remember what gets measured, gets achieved. By having oral and written updates, you can be assured that there is a likelihood of success in this particular license. The component is branding, where the licensee agrees to place the storage solutions logo on the covered products prior to shipping. The logo will be permanently displayed inside the product drawer or on a side panel. It is critical that the logo be placed on the product, and the licensee's agreement to follow through is placed in this particular contract.

**SPECIAL PROVISIONS/NOTES:**     Sales and Growth Initiatives:
Licensee agrees to provide Licensor with monthly updates both
orally (monthly update calls) and in writing (monthly Make Plan
Imperatives Report) during the course of the agreement.

Brand
Licensee agrees to permanently place the Storage Solutions logo
on the Covered Products prior to shipping. The logo will be
displayed inside the product i.e... in a drawer or on a side panel.

The last components of the Deal Term Sheet are the Standard Licensing Contract, the Credit Department Approval, and the Date Authorization needed. In the standard licensing contract section, "Yes" is selected. If it were not, you would have to explain why it wasn't selected and why senior management should approve it. For the Credit Department Approval, the answer is "Yes" again. Had the answer been no the likelihood of this getting approved would probably be low, but there could be extenuating circumstances that would justify this department doing so. Since this is a renewal the Date Authorization is needed as soon as possible. Once every area is completed, both you and the licensee can sign.

| | | | |
|---|---|---|---|
| **STANDARD LICENSING CONTRACT:** | Yes | X | No |
| **CREDIT DEPARTMENT APPROVAL:** | Yes | Per existing contract | No |
| **DATE AUTHORIZATION NEEDED:** | As soon as possible. | | |

_____
President, Excellent Cabinet, Inc.

_____
President, Storage Solutions, Inc.

Once the Deal Terms and Deal Term Sheets are approved and signed the contract is ready to be drafted. The standard provisions included in that contract include the following:

- Schedule A Standard terms and Conditions
- Schedule B Scope of Licensee
- Schedule C Royalty and Payment Terms
- Schedule D Submission Notice
- Schedule E Manufacturer Agreement
- Schedule F Quality Standard

This concludes this section of our presentation. Ready for the next section? If so, let's begin.

# Chapter 11
# Negotiating Contract - Part 2

In Part I of Negotiating Contract, the focused was set on Agreeing Deal Terms and getting the Internal Approval Sheet approved. Once both you and the Manufacturer approve the memo, Part II can begin. Part II will discuss what Standard Terms and Conditions are included in the contract and how correctly structuring the agreement will lead to an executed agreement, i.e., signed by both parties.

Schedule A is the **Standard Contract Terms and Conditions** and includes thirty sections that cover every component of the licensing agreement. The first section is the **Definitions** section, which entails everything from what it means to have an affiliate authorization channel, Royalty Rates, Commercialization Date, covered products, and the list continues. The definition section is crucial because it helps everyone who reviews it to understand the specific terms of the agreement. One term that is critical to the overall contract is Net Sales. The Net Sales figures are multiplied by the Royalty Rate to determine the amount of royalty that has to be paid. This is why having an understanding of Net Sales is so critical!

The second section is **License Granted.** As mentioned in part one of the section, Negotiating Contract, most contracts are non-exclusive. In our example, non-exclusivity is the default. It also delineates information related to the trademark and where the licensee can and cannot use the trademark.

The third section has to do with **Quality Control and Compliance Laws.** These are relatively straightforward, so I will not elaborate on them here. The fourth section, **Approvals,** is a critical part of the overall program for you and the licensee to understand. In this section, you should address: What is the Approval Process? When do we create a new concept? How long does it take to get the concept approved? What does the Approval Process look like for the prototype and the final production stages? Additionally you, the Licensing Team, the Brand Manager, and the Product Manager should be knowledgeable about the licensee's responsibilities. Understanding these will make it simpler when you collaborate with the licensee, helping to ensure a successful program.

The fifth section is **Royalty Payments**; this section provides information about how the royalty payments are calculated, when they have to be paid, and what are the Advances the licensee has to pay. The specifics of these aspects of the areas are defined here; they are referenced in Schedule B and Schedule C as well.

The sixth section deals with **Records and Auditing**. In this section, it states that the licensee has to keep records of everything they've sold and that you, as the brand owner, have the right to audit that information on a periodic basis to make sure that what is being reported is accurate. If you have a good relationship with the licensee, the language in this section will never need to be invoked other than for standard routine reasons; however, if the relationship becomes strained and the program goals aren't achieved, you might request that an audit take place. The seventh section centers on **Trademark Rights and Work Product**. This declares that the trademark is owned by you, the licensor, and will always be owned by you. In almost in every case you will own any Work Product under this agreement that's been developed by the licensee. It's important that the licensee realizes before they sign the agreement that what they create will transfer ownership to the licensor.

**Marketing and Sales** is the eighth section of the contract and is a valuable component of the licensing agreement. This section explains what is required by the licensee in the area of marketing and sales to ensure success.

The **Term** of the agreement is laid out in the ninth section and details explicitly when this agreement shall begin and end as well as any provisions related to the agreement. This section may even include extensions. An example of the importance of clarity on term can be seen from a case study regarding

Kraft and Starbucks. In 2010, Kraft was selling Starbucks branded coffee in retail and grocery channels as an official licensee of Starbucks. Starbucks terminated that agreement because they wanted to use a third-party manufacturer to produce and sell coffee on their behalf. Kraft argued that they held a perpetual license to the Starbucks brand and therefore, Starbucks' termination of their license was not legal. In the Starbucks- Kraft license example, the attorney's from both sides would have reviewed the section of their agreement covering the Term to determine if Kraft's claim to a "perpetual" license was legitimate. Usually, every agreement has a term that can expire and or be renewed. Without having read Usually, every agreement has a term that can expire and or be renewed. Without having read the agreement, it is hard for me to say if their contract was perpetual, but from the looks of what was reported by Kraft there was a reference to automatic renewals in their contract.

The Starbucks – Kraft license example presents an excellent segue to the tenth section of the Standard Terms & Conditions of the Licensing Contract, **Termination**. In any licensing contract the question "When can this contract be terminated?" always arises. Typically, the termination section is heavily weighted towards you, as the licensor, because you are charged with protecting the brand. Using this section to enforce termination rights will ensure the safety of your brand. It is important to emphasize to the licensee that if the contract is not followed to the letter any breaches, such as not following the approval process or not following the contract in general, might result in termination of the agreement. All of the pitfalls discussed in Chapter 3 come to mind when we consider termination. As if termination wasn't painful enough for the licensee, a licensee whose contract is terminated may be subject to penalties based on the reason for the termination, as stated in this particular section.

**Effect of Termination or Expiration** is covered in the eleventh section. This mainly addresses what happens if the contract is terminated. The twelfth section, Representations and Warranties, articulate what you are contractually representing as the licensor and licensee respectively. Simply stated these are what you represent and what you warranty, i.e., your beliefs. Both of these sections should be a straightforward part of the agreement.

The thirteenth section, **Indemnification**, states if one party does something that is not correct or not legal they indemnify the other party and vice versa. This means you are not liable for actions taken by the other party that may not comply with laws and regulations. The fourteenth section focuses on **Infringement By Third Parties.** This section determines what happens in infringement cases and how both companies will notify the other and work together to get those issues resolved. You and the licensee should support one another in ensuring that no third-party can infringe on this agreement. For example, there might be a particular case where another manufacturer illegally makes use of the rights on the brand. If this were to happen and the licensee learns about it, they should report it to you. You should then immediately notify your counsel so they can contact the third party to stop the infringement.

The **Insurance** section discusses the provisions that are required in the fifteenth section. This will clearly state how much insurance is required and the term that insurance is required. Most licenses require the products be insured for up to five years after the contract is terminated or expires. Depending on the particular category, the term can be as many as ten years after termination or expiration. **Confidential** information is covered in the sixteenth section. Confidential information represents any information that might hurt either party if it is exposed in the marketplace. This section specifies how each company is to protect the other's confidential information.

In the seventeenth section, **Manufacturing and Authorized Manufacturers** explain how a third-party may manufacture on behalf of the licensee. The eighteenth section has to do with **Unfair Labor Practices and Human Rights Laws.** Typically as the brand owner, you will require that the licensee ensure that no unfair labor practices occur in the manufacturing of their product. So that means no slave labor, no child labor, or anything along this line that can hurt the brand. The unfair labor practices are covered here to warrant the brand is protected.

In the nineteenth section, the **Press Releases** are the focal point. Make note that if a licensee wants to issue a press release about your license they have to ask your permission. The twentieth section's main topic is about **Customer Service**. Customer service is important for both parties, but as the brand owner, you want to know that the customer service is going to be handled in a very forthright and efficient manner. You will need to lay out the criteria that are required in order for your brand's promise to be met. This normally includes citing a way to contact the licensee from the website and listing a toll-free number for a consumer or customer to voice a complaint or make an inquiry. This section also includes what procedures and policies will be enacted as it relates to how the licensee will follow up with someone who makes a complaint. **Identification of Licensee and Use of Licensee's Name** is displayed in the twenty-first section of the agreement. You and the licensee provide these details.

The twenty-second section addresses **Assignability and Change in Control.** This can include when the licensee wants to assign the license they have acquired from you to a new owner due to a change in organizational structure. It's a very basic provision. Just include how the notices should be formatted and where any information or updates should be sent.

The twenty-third section focuses on **Notices**. This specifies that all notices and statements must be presented in writing, and delivered at the respective addresses of the designated parties. If, however, there is a change in address the recipient must provide this in writing before notices and statement are delivered to the address provided. A stipulation that a copy of all notices to the licensor shall be sent to a specific destination is also included for this notice to be effective.

The twenty-fourth section addresses **Force Majeure**. This typically refers to what are known as Acts of God. If, for example, there is a flood, an earthquake or a volcanic eruption that affects the ability to commercialize the business then this section holds the provisions to allow for such occurrence.

Once things settle back down, business will continue as usual. The twenty-fifth section discusses the **Waiver** in case of any breach of a provision. In the twenty- sixth section **Severability** is the main topic. Severability means that if the contract is deemed to have a portion that is not legal, it doesn't affect the rest of the agreement. The agreement doesn't, in other words, become void just because one section might be.

**Governing Law** is addressed in the twenty-seventh section. Almost every time, if not every time, the governing law will be that of the country or state where you, the licensor, have your headquarters. You are the one who is driving this agreement. For instances, if your business is in California, but the licensee business is in New York, then the governing law will take place in California. The laws of California will apply if there is ever a lawsuit impacted by this agreement. In the twenty-eighth section, **No Agency Created** explains that if both parties are working together no entity would be created outside of the relationship that you have. The twenty-ninth section refers to the **Survivable Provisions**. In other words, after the agreement is over these are the section(s) that still lives on after the agreement is retired. These are the sections that remain relevant post expiration or termination. Finally, the thirtieth section addresses **Counterparts**. It is the legal relationship between the parties as it relates to this particular agreement. Again, this is a standard provision that is found in almost every agreement.

So that is the total summary of the provisions of the Standard Contract Terms and Conditions. Now I would like to address what is required internally if the level of the value of a particular contract reaches a certain limit, e.g., $1M in Net Present Value. Oftentimes it is required to send a memo to the Chief Executive Officer about the agreement that stipulates why he or she should agree to sign the license. When this occurs, a memo outlining the details of the licensing agreement may be required and the sections of this memo would include something like this:

- First, can the licensee deliver reliable quality and service levels? That's very important to any business and that should be addressed in the memo.

- Second, how will the license help the brand? Again, it always goes back to how do you reinforce your strength of the brand in its core component or capability.
- Third, does the financial return justify our time and total effort?

Hallelujah! Everything is approved; the contract is signed; handshakes are made; toasts are made, and now the hard work begins. Now that the contract is signed and the agreement is completed, it is time to move into the final two phases, which deal with **Orientation and Business Planning.**

In summary, when you are signing the contract the first step is to Agree Deal Terms. Next you want to sign the Deal Term Summary, and then you want to finalize the Deal Term Sheet. The information provided in this term sheet is then moved over into a contract, which is the negotiation piece. Once that contract is laid out with the lawyers then you will review all the steps and make sure that all the language is agreeable. Any terms that need to get modified should be modified in that phase. Finally, if there is a memo required to the CEO because of the size of the deal, you cover those provisions in the memo. The CEO approves the deal and then finally the contract is signed. The contract is then ready to be initiated, and the program can begin. That completes this particular section.

# Chapter 12
# Conducting Orientation

Well done! Negotiations have been made, and the contract has been signed. The execution of the contract signifies the beginning of the relationship. It is, therefore, the licensor's responsibility to ensure that they provide the licensee with the information they need to be successful. In Chapter 12 the licensor will learn about the **Conducting Orientation** phase and the **Approval Process**, and how important these components are in the success of a long-lasting licensing program, starting with how to properly and effectively conduct an orientation.

Not long after the contract has been signed it is time to include a formal Orientation session, but why is an orientation session relevant to the brand licensing program? Well, there are countless reasons why conducting an Orientation is essential, but the most important is it helps build an ongoing relationship between you and the manufacturer. Another reason is that there are a whole host of requirements that make the program successful. It takes everything from understanding the brand to getting the products approved, to commercializing the product in the marketplace. This requires a great deal of personnel from both you and licensee side to know what that agreement means, and the **Orientation Process** allows for both parties to grasp this understanding.

The licensees are responsible for the most crucial asset of your company, which is the brand. Therefore, you want to ensure that the brand is in good hands. You must know that the manufacturer has a deep understanding of the brand. As a brand owner, you also want to know that the manufacturer will build the attributes of the brand into their products, obtain the Approvals in the right way, and follow the guidelines. The Orientation Process ensures the commercialization in the category takes place. You will now be able to see new officially licensed products in the marketplace that consumers crave. Finally, the Orientation Process ensures that the licensee meets and exceeds the contract obligations. You don't just want the licensee to hit Minimum

Guarantees; they should be hitting your mutually agreed Sales Targets and the corresponding Royalties to increase the overall success of the license.

So, what is the goal of the Orientation Process? It aids in the long-term success of the partnership from its very outset. Everybody would agree that you have made a tremendous investment up to this point and because of such an investment; you want to see the payoff. The Orientation Process helps get that started. You have to achieve this by (1) ***Identifying Roles and Responsibilities of the parties on the licensor side and the licensee side;*** (2) ***get everyone up to speed on the obligations, and*** (3) ***ensure the parties on both sides know each other and their respective roles.*** Up to this point, maybe one or two people have had a certain depth of knowledge about what has happened and what has been required, but now you have to get all those parties and all those different departments within both companies aligned, up to speed, and ready to go.

As the Orientation Process progresses, you will want to then discuss your roles and responsibilities as the licensor. This is the time to specify the responsibilities of the Licensing Team and the Business Unit to ensure a successful licensing agreement.

<u>**The Licensing Team roles include the following:**</u>
- Recommend product categories
- Develop licensing plan to support business strategy
- Identify potential partners
- Conduct due diligence
- Negotiate inbound (acquiring a brand to be placed on your product) licensing deals
- Negotiate outbound (allowing your brand to be used by another company) licensing deals
- Ensure contract compliance
- Manage approval process
- Manage licensees and licensing agencies
- Managing financial forecast

**The Business Unit roles include the following:**
- Provide brand platforms
- Recommend product categories (research, gain consumer permission, decide licensing category)
- Identify potential partners
- Develop brand strategy and business plan
- Approve deals to ensure alignment
- Approve and provide input on packaging and product development (critical to share with licensee)
- Integrate retail sales team
- Track brand and consumer metrics

On **Orientation Day**, you are able to have a face-to-face conversation with the licensee. At this point, both you and the licensee ought to be thinking about what the obligations are and how you're going to work together. The Orientation Day is designed to summarize all of this information and make sure that everyone who is responsible or will be responsible for the contract is up-to-date on his or her obligations. What will happen in the face-to-face meeting is that you and the licensee will exchange business cards, give handshakes, get to know each other, and start understanding what is important. Understanding who should attend the Orientation is crucial. Attendees from your (the licensor's) side should include, at minimum, Members of The Licensing Group, the Brand Group, Product Development, and Sales. These are all the members of the organization that are going to have an impact on the licensee and are going to be responsible for certain aspects of the contract. The licensee should send their General Manager, and if possible, Product Development, Account Management, and Sales and Marketing Representatives. Take this time to align the senior management and also inform the junior personnel on what is required on a day-to-day basis. If all of the right people are at the Orientation, everyone should receive the information needed, and the program is going to start off strong.

Not only is it important to know which members of each organization should be in attendance, but also it is equally important for both parties to understand what to bring to the orientation. Your side should bring your company overview. Make sure that members on the licensee side are knowledgeable about your company's mission and vision, where you intend to go and what you believe. Give an overview of the brand. This should include the Brand Essence, the Brand Architecture, and the Brand Style Guide. Consider also providing information on how you handle packaging and labeling, you testing protocols and your contract structure. This gives you a chance to go through the contract at some level of detail, so the licensee's side knows where to reference the contract when they have a question.

On the licensee side, they should bring a Company Overview also which states who they are, what they stand for, why they are here, and why they want the license. Then the licensee should give a Sales Overview that includes the specified channels, the retailers, and how are they will promote your business and their business with your brand. A Marketing Overview should also be given to show you how they will use marketing dollars to grow this business, grow the category, and expand your brand in this particular category. Once completed the licensee's Development Team should go through their overview of how they develop products and how they use innovation in product development to grow the company. The Product Development Team should bring sample products so that you can visualize what they are talking about and planning to develop over the term of the contract. You will either meet these briefings with positive reactions showing they really understand it or if there are any issues they can be addressed right out of the gates. Finally, the licensee should bring concept designs on where they intend to go with the product to get your input and opinion.

You along with the licensee should also come prepared with topics of discussion. Topics can include Contract Terms and Business Implications, Brand and Category Strategy, Brand Guidelines, the Approval Process, Testing, and even Audit Protocols. Contract terms should cover the Covered Products, the Authorized Channels, the Territories, Quality Compliance, Approvals, Work Product, Customer Service, Trademark Right, Trademark Notices, and the Manufacturer's Authorization Agreement. When that's finished, you will be putting yourself in position for success. All who are present will be exposed to those particular requirements and have a good understanding of where they need to go. From a Brand and Category Strategy perspective, your focus should center on the target market and the Brand Positioning in addition to the Category Positioning. Don't forget that the Category Positioning has to be aligned with the Brand Positioning. Then touch on building the brand attributes into the product to support the category. See if the product passes the Litmus test. If you were to pull the logo off the product would consumers still be able to recognize what brand is being represented?

Here are some examples of the two product guidelines: Product Style Guide and Packaging Style Guide.

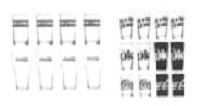 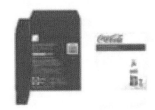 

*Product and Packaging Style Guide*

When looking at the Coca-Cola example above, you can see the representation of what is included in a particular Style Guide. That's the kind of detail that you want to require to be made for this particular category and should already been made. If it isn't created, this level of detail is what you need to be sharing with the licensee on the day of the Orientation. Typically, the product guidelines are provided in both physical and digital form. A digital form is more important because the designers from the licensing team will need to pull all those digital elements and put them on the product and packaging.

***

Now let's review the **Approval Process.** Looking at figure 12-1 you can see that the Approval Process starts with the Licensee who will send information to the Licensing Coordinator on your team. The Licensing Coordinator will then send the information to the Product Design Alignment, the Graphic Design Alignment, and the Quality & Safety Alignment teams. While this provides an overview of the process, it is vital for you to know what each process entails so let's look at the three-stage process in more detail.

## Approval Process

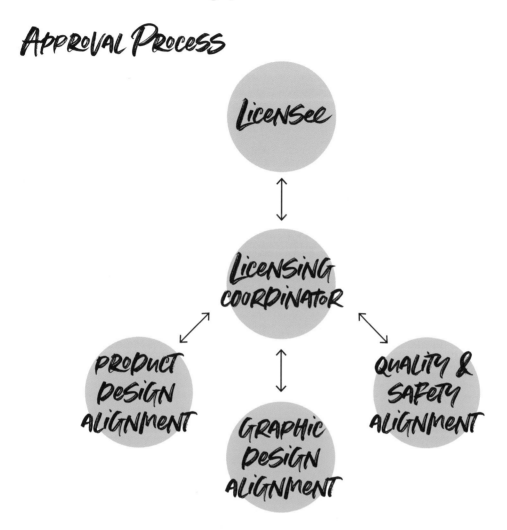

*Figure 12-1 Approval Process*

There are three phases of any particular Approval Process: the Concept, the Prototype, and the Final Production Run. The Concept represents a two-dimensional design of what the product should look like. You will review the product positioning, industrial design language, the graphic design, and the engineering review of the quality standards. If all those criteria are met on the Concept, then the Concept stage is approved. This is more than just a cursory review and an approval. There is a significant amount of review that takes place in this section of the Approval Process.

The Prototype is a three-dimensional physical example of what the product should resemble. In this phase, you will review industrial design language, the graphic design, the packaging; moreover, the engineering team evaluates the Prototype. This is similar to the Concept Approval Process, but you will be reviewing a physical product rather than an image. Again, this is a significant detailed review to make sure that the Prototype physically looks right, to determine if the product can perform the role it's supposed to perform and has all the design elements built into the product. Once this phase is approved, it goes to the final approval stage. Before final approval safety testing must take place. This is to ensure that the product meets the standards outlined in the contract. The safety standards are given by you or by a third-party representative, such as a Bureau Veritas (well known for their testing protocols and standards) who understands what the safety standards should be for every product category in the marketplace.

The last phase is the Final Production Run. In this stage the product should look exactly like the Prototype you saw in the Prototype phase, and every one after that should look like the Prototype. Once the final review of the product is completed, and the results of the testing are satisfied the product can enter the marketplace.

Here is a timeline of the Approval Process.

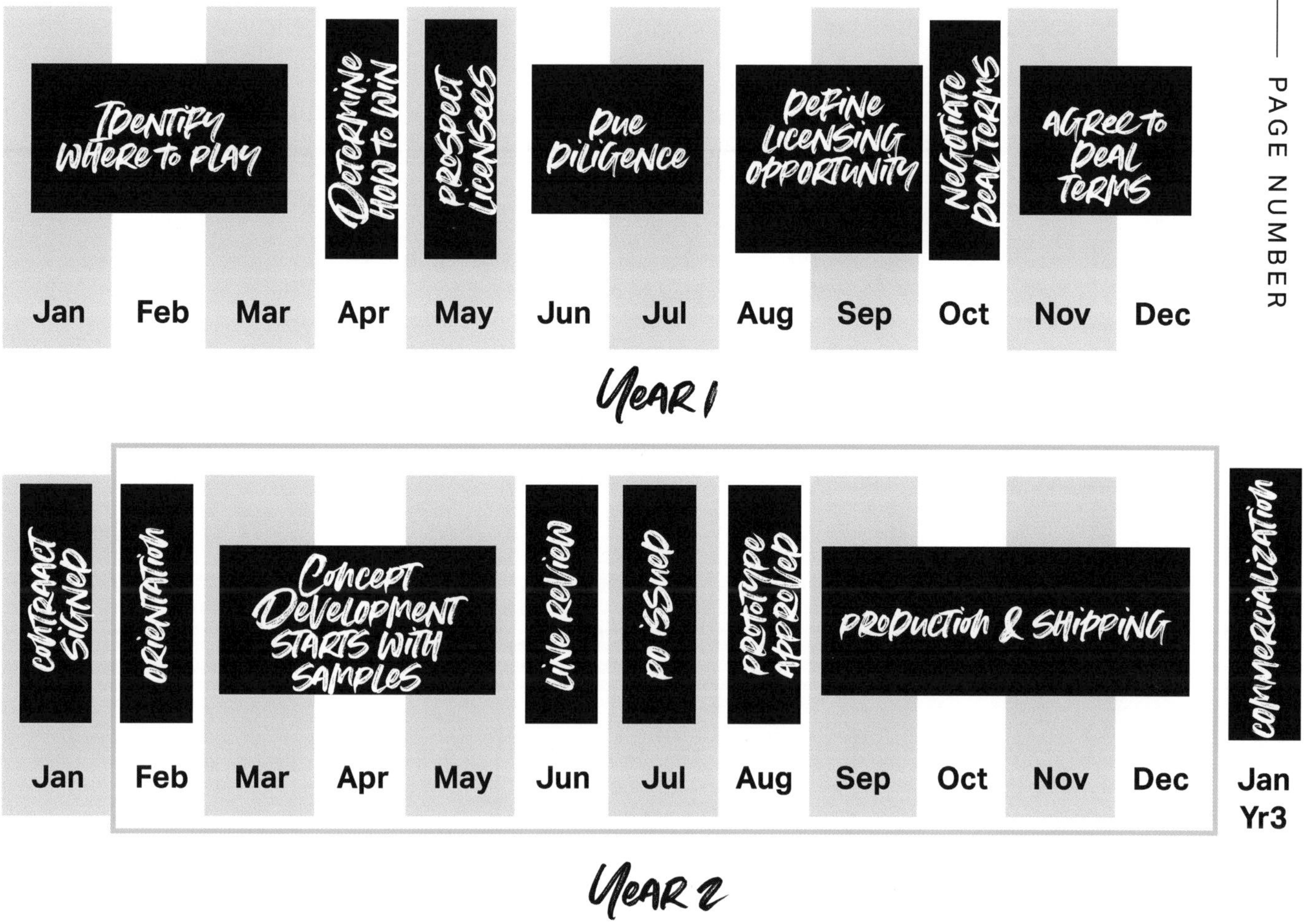

Figure 12-3 Approval Process Timeline

Between February and May of Year 2 is where this Approval Process takes place after the contract is signed. Once the Orientation Team is set, and all of these steps are followed, you are set up for success in your licensing program.

"Built to Last" is another way to look at the Approval Process. On the left-hand side of Figure 12-2, you can see there is graphic design style guideline, industrial guidelines, quality and safety standards, licensing category strategy, and contract rights. This diagram is designed to show you that if each of these elements to the left of the diagram are covered, and you complete the three-stage process (the Concept stage, Prototype stage, and the Final Production Run stage) while course correcting along the way, you are going to deliver a product in the marketplace that is best-in-class, builds the brand attributes into the product, reinforces the brand, and satisfies the consumer, retailers, manufacturers, and yourself.

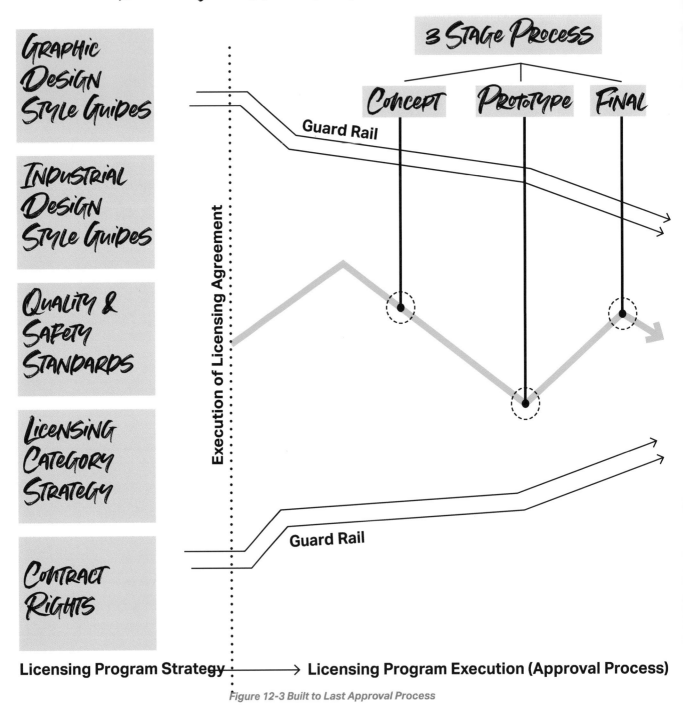

Figure 12-3 Built to Last Approval Process

Before ending this section, I want to mention Testing and Audit Protocols. These are two more critical components of the contract that need to be discussed. As mentioned earlier, testing protocols are driven by company standards or third-party standards. Quality and safety standards include routine site visits at manufacturing facilities, supplier and manufacturer approvals, safety and social compliance audits, and finally QA report cards. This is a very important piece because what is being made has to be approved and has to be made right. You cannot allow for any provision that can hurt the brand, the product, and most importantly the consumer.

That concludes the section on the orientation process. Our next and final piece will be on business planning.

# Chapter 13

# Establishing Business Plan

Congratulations! You have reached the final chapter of our process, **"Establishing Business Plan."** The business plan created is a critical component in ensuring the success of your program. When you work side-by-side with the licensee and monitor the success of their business with your brand in the marketplace, you will enhance your success. In this final chapter, you will learn how to understand your licensee's business plans and ensure alignment with your own business objectives to develop steps towards success.

Once you have signed the contract and made sure the licensee has a good understanding of the brand, it is essential to give the license the right tools to be successful. Monitoring the licensee's business and ensuring that they set achievable targets empowers the licensee to maximize the license. From a business planning perspective, this entails **Sales Management**, Marketing Management, and Quality and Compliance Management. Sales Management business planning can be broken down into annual, quarterly, or monthly business plans. An Annual Business Plan traditionally gets developed in the third-quarter of the prior year to the next year's business plan. While Sales Management business planning can be broken down into quarters, the **Marketing Management** planning is generally created as an annual business plan. In this Annual Business Plan, the licensee should explain what they intend to do with the brand in that category, what they are going to spend to achieve their goals and how they will align the marketing mix with your own brand marketing. Once discussed, they should then agree to the budget, and how the budget will be spent. **Quality and Compliance Management** is neither broken down quarterly or annually; it's an ongoing planning that never ends. This critical piece makes sure that the quality of the products improves or is maintained through an ongoing program that's established by the licensee's quality team on a daily or weekly basis.

The Annual Business Plan, for the licensee is also typically developed in the third-quarter of the year prior to when the plan is being invoked. Once developed it will be reviewed by the key management team of the licensee and then shared with you and your team. The materials that are included in this plan are traditionally what are included in any business plan. The template provided will share the minimum requirements needed to ensure success. The key elements included in this Annual Business Plan are Sales Forecast, Royalty Forecast, Line Review Dates, and other Key Retailer Dates. The Sales and Royalty Forecasts are represented by region, channel, and product. Line Review Dates focus on the dates that the licensee will meet with the retailer to discuss the products and sales. The Key Retailer Dates include major presentations, initiatives that are being done, and innovative products that they should consider as part of their updated modular set in the ongoing sales of your licensed product in their stores. Below is a snapshot of the **Annual Business Plan.**

## Annual Business Plan

| | | | |
|---|---|---|---|
| Licensee Name | Licensee #1 | Year 2 Licensor Budget: | 3,000,000 |
| Submission Date: | Year 2 | Year 2 Licensee Budget: | 350,000 |
| Royalty Rates (%): | 5, 7.5, 10 | Licensee Contribution: | 12% |
| Minimum Guarantees: | 100,000 | | |
| | | Year 2 Licensor Estimate: | 3,500,000 |
| | | Year 2 Licensee Estimate: | 375,000 |
| | | Licensee Contribution: | 11% |

*PAGE NUMBER*

### Sales & Royalty Summary Goal

| | Year 1 | Year 2 | | Comparison | |
|---|---|---|---|---|---|
| | Actual | Budget | Estimate | Yr 1 Actual vs. Yr 2 Budget | Yr 2 Budget vs. Estimate |
| Sales | 2,500,000 | 3,500,000 | 3,750,000 | 40% | 7% |
| Royalites | 250,000 | 350,000 | 375,000 | 40% | 7% |

### Retailer Summary Goal

| Retailer | Year 1 | | Year 2 | | |
|---|---|---|---|---|---|
| | Sales | Royalties | Sales | Royalties | % of Estimate |
| Wal-Mart | 658,000 | 65,800 | 770,000 | 77,000 | 21% |
| Target | 475,000 | 47,500 | 573,000 | 57,300 | 15% |
| The Home Depot | 378,000 | 37,800 | 425,000 | 42,500 | 11% |
| Lowe's | 299,000 | 29,900 | 411,000 | 41,100 | 11% |
| SAM's Club | 108,000 | 10,800 | 379,000 | 37,900 | 10% |
| Costco | 107,000 | 10,700 | 368,000 | 36,800 | 10% |
| SEARS | 97,000 | 9,700 | 320,000 | 32,000 | 9% |
| Kmart | 75,000 | 7,500 | 144,000 | 14,400 | 4% |
| Kohl's | 55,000 | 5,500 | 110,000 | 11,000 | 3% |
| Other | 248,000 | 24,800 | 250,000 | 25,000 | 7% |
| Total | 2,500,000 | 250,000 | 3,750,000 | 375,000 | 100% |

### Product Summary Goal

| Product | Year 1 | | Year 2 | | |
|---|---|---|---|---|---|
| | Sales | Royalties | Sales | Royalties | % of Estimate |
| A | 658,000 | 65,800 | 770,000 | 77,000 | 21% |
| B | 475,000 | 47,500 | 573,000 | 57,300 | 15% |
| C | 378,000 | 37,800 | 425,000 | 42,500 | 11% |
| D | 299,000 | 29,900 | 411,000 | 41,100 | 11% |
| E | 108,000 | 10,800 | 379,000 | 37,900 | 10% |
| F | 107,000 | 10,700 | 368,000 | 36,800 | 10% |
| G | 97,000 | 9,700 | 320,000 | 32,000 | 9% |
| H | 75,000 | 7,500 | 144,000 | 14,400 | 4% |
| I | 55,000 | 5,500 | 110,000 | 11,000 | 3% |
| J | 248,000 | 24,800 | 250,000 | 25,000 | 7% |
| Total | 2,500,000 | 250,000 | 3,750,000 | 375,000 | 100% |

*Figure 13-1: Annual Business Plan*

**Sales & Royalty Summary Stretch**

| | Year 1 | Year 2 | | Comparison | |
|---|---|---|---|---|---|
| | Actual | Budget | Estimate | Yr 1 Actual vs. Yr 2 Budget | Yr 2 Budget vs. Estimate |
| Sales | 2,500,000 | 3,500,000 | 3,750,000 | 40% | 7% |
| Royalites | 250,000 | 350,000 | 375,000 | 40% | 7% |

**Retailer Summary Stretch**

| | Year 1 | | Year 2 | | |
|---|---|---|---|---|---|
| Retailer | Sales | Royalties | Sales | Royalties | % of Estimate |
| Wal-Mart | 658,000 | 65,800 | 1,000,000 | 77,000 | 21% |
| Target | 475,000 | 47,500 | 700,000 | 57,300 | 15% |
| The Home Depot | 378,000 | 37,800 | 450,000 | 42,500 | 11% |
| Lowe's | 299,000 | 29,900 | 425,000 | 41,100 | 11% |
| SAM's Club | 108,000 | 10,800 | 379,000 | 37,900 | 10% |
| Costco | 107,000 | 10,700 | 368,000 | 36,800 | 10% |
| SEARS | 97,000 | 9,700 | 320,000 | 32,000 | 9% |
| Kmart | 75,000 | 7,500 | 144,000 | 14,400 | 4% |
| Kohl's | 55,000 | 5,500 | 110,000 | 11,000 | 3% |
| Other | 248,000 | 24,800 | 250,000 | 25,000 | 7% |
| Total | 2,500,000 | 250,000 | 4,186,000 | 375,000 | 100% |

**Product Summary Stretch**

| | Year 1 | | Year 2 | | |
|---|---|---|---|---|---|
| Product | Sales | Royalties | Sales | Royalties | % of Estimate |
| A | 658,000 | 65,800 | 900,000 | 77,000 | 21% |
| B | 475,000 | 47,500 | 573,000 | 57,300 | 15% |
| C | 378,000 | 37,800 | 425,000 | 42,500 | 11% |
| D | 299,000 | 29,900 | 500,000 | 41,100 | 11% |
| E | 108,000 | 10,800 | 379,000 | 37,900 | 10% |
| F | 107,000 | 10,700 | 468,000 | 36,800 | 10% |
| G | 97,000 | 9,700 | 320,000 | 32,000 | 9% |
| H | 75,000 | 7,500 | 144,000 | 14,400 | 4% |
| | 55,000 | 5,500 | 227,000 | 11,000 | 3% |
| J | 248,000 | 24,800 | 250,000 | 25,000 | 7% |
| Total | 2,500,000 | 250,000 | 4,186,000 | 375,000 | 100% |

*Figure 13-1: Annual Business Plan (continued)*

As you can see, there is a lot involved with the business plan, so let's look at each section in detail to understand what exactly is expected from each party. Even though you are not developing the Annual Business Plan, it is still vital that you understand what it involves. The first section of the Annual Business Plan requests:

- The licensee's name
- The submission date
- The royalty rates
- The minimum guaranteed royalties for the year
- The licensor's budget
- The licensee's budget
- The licensee's contributions (budget)
- The licensor's estimate
- The licensee's estimate
- The licensee's contributions (estimate)

### Annual Business Plan

| | | | |
|---|---|---|---|
| Licensee Name | Licensee #1 | Year 2 Licensor Budget: | 3,000,000 |
| Submission Date: | Year 2 | Year 2 Licensee Budget: | 350,000 |
| Royalty Rates (%): | 5, 7.5, 10 | Licensee Contribution: | 12% |
| Minimum Guarantees: | 100,000 | | |
| | | Year 2 Licensor Estimate: | 3,500,000 |
| | | Year 2 Licensee Estimate: | 375,000 |
| | | Licensee Contribution: | 11% |

Take a look at the estimates above; did you notice that the estimates relate to the budget? In this particular example, this plan was submitted in Year 2 of the contract; the royalty rates were 5 percent, 7.5 percent, and 10 percent, and the Minimum Guarantee Royalty was a $100,000. The licensor's budget for the total business plan was $3M; the licensee's budget was $350,000, which represented 12 percent of the overall licensor's budget. This percentage shows the significance of this program. The licensor's estimate for the Year 2 is $3.5M and the licensees estimate $375,000. In both these cases, they are estimated to exceed their budget amount for Year 1. The contribution is 11 percent, which is a bit lower percentage then the budgeted percentage of 12 percent.

When looking at the **Sales and Royalty Summary Goal** below, what you see is the actual numbers in Year 1 were $2.5M for the licensor and $250,000 in royalties. For Year 2, there was $3.5M for the budget, and the royalties were $350,000. The estimate is $3.75M at a 10 percent royalty rate, which equals $375,000. In Year 2 the *actual budget* vs. the *estimated budget* is compared and shows an increased by 40 percent. The actual budget vs. the estimate budget also shows a difference of 7 percent. This is the kind of high-level detail you want in a business plan to know how you faring compared to where you were in the previous year.

### Sales & Royalty Summary Goal

|  | Year 1 | Year 2 | | Comparison | |
|  |  |  |  | Yr 1 Actual vs. | Yr 2 Budget vs. |
|  | Actual | Budget | Estimate | Yr 2 Budget | Estimate |
| Sales | 2,500,000 | 3,500,000 | 3,750,000 | 40% | 7% |
| Royalites | 250,000 | 350,000 | 375,000 | 40% | 7% |

The **Retailer Summary Goal** by retailer is the next section to consider. In this particular case, all the retailers are listed on the left-hand side by the total number of sales projected. Starting with Walmart and ending with Kohl's you see $658,000 in sales in Year 1 all the way down to 55,000 for Kohl's with Other at $248,000. The royalties correlated with that at 10 percent royalty rate is $250,000 on a base of $2.5 M in sales. In Year 2, Walmart's amount is $770,000, and the total for the whole projection $3.75M. The royalties generated are $375,000 in total, and the estimated percentage per retailer is outlined on the right-hand side with Walmart at 21 percent all the way down to 3 percent for Kohl's; this totals to 100 percent for the royalties that are projected.

**Retailer Summary Goal**

| Retailer | Year 1 | | Year 2 | | |
|---|---|---|---|---|---|
| | Sales | Royalties | Sales | Royalties | % of Estimate |
| Wal-Mart | 658,000 | 65,800 | 770,000 | 77,000 | 21% |
| Target | 475,000 | 47,500 | 573,000 | 57,300 | 15% |
| The Home Depot | 378,000 | 37,800 | 425,000 | 42,500 | 11% |
| Lowe's | 299,000 | 29,900 | 411,000 | 41,100 | 11% |
| SAM's Club | 108,000 | 10,800 | 379,000 | 37,900 | 10% |
| Costco | 107,000 | 10,700 | 368,000 | 36,800 | 10% |
| SEARS | 97,000 | 9,700 | 320,000 | 32,000 | 9% |
| Kmart | 75,000 | 7,500 | 144,000 | 14,400 | 4% |
| Kohl's | 55,000 | 5,500 | 110,000 | 11,000 | 3% |
| Other | 248,000 | 24,800 | 250,000 | 25,000 | 7% |
| Total | 2,500,000 | 250,000 | 3,750,000 | 375,000 | 100% |

In the next section of the Annual Business Plan is the **Product Summary Goal.** For the sake of simplicity, the letters A–J identifies the products. The sales are broken down in Year 1 similar to the retailer component and go from the largest to smallest in product percentages. Then Year 1 is compared to the Year 2 sales to provide a cross-reference between the retailers and the products in order for you to see how the whole mix is completed and how it makes up 100 percent of the total sales that are going to be made.

**Product Summary Goal**

| Product | Year 1 | | Year 2 | | |
|---|---|---|---|---|---|
| | Sales | Royalties | Sales | Royalties | % of Estimate |
| A | 658,000 | 65,800 | 770,000 | 77,000 | 21% |
| B | 475,000 | 47,500 | 573,000 | 57,300 | 15% |
| C | 378,000 | 37,800 | 425,000 | 42,500 | 11% |
| D | 299,000 | 29,900 | 411,000 | 41,100 | 11% |
| E | 108,000 | 10,800 | 379,000 | 37,900 | 10% |
| F | 107,000 | 10,700 | 368,000 | 36,800 | 10% |
| G | 97,000 | 9,700 | 320,000 | 32,000 | 9% |
| H | 75,000 | 7,500 | 144,000 | 14,400 | 4% |
| I | 55,000 | 5,500 | 110,000 | 11,000 | 3% |
| J | 248,000 | 24,800 | 250,000 | 25,000 | 7% |
| Total | 2,500,000 | 250,000 | 3,750,000 | 375,000 | 100% |

Moving along, the **Key Retailer Dates** will be the last section of the Annual Business Plan. This section provides the licensee's key dates for when the licensee will meet with the retailers. The Key Retailer Dates should also contain the detail of summary numbers to create a better understanding of the overall size of the program. As you reference a specific retailer line review, you want to outline the retailers. As the brand owner, you want to know the following about the products: What products are the licensee going to be selling? What line reviews dates are there? When is the licensee going to be bringing those products in the review with the buyers and getting purchase orders from those line reviews? Similarly, the licensee may have other meetings that you should also be aware of that may involve new product innovations, new marketing initiatives, and new customer service procedures. These meeting can also be designated by the retailer asking the licensee to come in to disseminate the information that is important to them including service abilities, standards, and so forth. Having these dates on the business plan will inform you about what is upcoming.

### Licensee Key Dates

| Licensee Name | Licensee #1 | Year 1 Licensor Budget: | 3,000,000 |
|---|---|---|---|
| Submission Date: | Year 1 | Year 1 Licensee Budget: | 350,000 |
| Royalty Rates (%): | 5, 7.5, 10 | Licensee Contribution: | 12% |
| Minimum Guarantees: | 100,000 | | |
| | | Year 1 Licensor Estimate: | 3,500,000 |
| | | Year 1 Licensee Estimate: | 375,000 |
| | | Licensee Contribution: | 11% |

### Retailer Line Reviews

| Retailer | Products | Line Review Date |
|---|---|---|
| Wal-Mart | | |
| Target | | |
| The Home Depot | | |
| Lowe's | | |
| SAM's Club | | |
| Costco | | |
| SEARS | | |
| Kmart | | |
| Kohl's | | |

**"Other" Retailer Meetings**

| Retailer | Products | Line Review Date |
|----------|----------|------------------|
| Wal-Mart | | |
| Target | | |
| The Home Depot | | |
| Lowe's | | |
| SAM's Club | | |
| Costco | | |
| SEARS | | |
| Kmart | | |
| Kohl's | | |

Now it's time to look at the sales planning from a Quarterly Business Plan perspective. The Quarterly Business Plan discusses:

- Previous quarter meetings with the retailers and results
- Upcoming meetings
- Actual vs. Estimates vs. Budget for Sales and Royalties
  - How did we do vs. the estimate?
  - How did we do vs. the budget?
- Roadblocks to success
- Key elements to win

Since the budget component contains a bit more information, let's review them in detail. For example, if the budget is set in Month 9, what will be seen in the calendar year is an updated estimate that is provided every month. The actuals (Sales Recognized) are provided at the end of each month and can be revised to the budget numbers to include additional information that may impact the overall sales. This can include a new product that is going to market that is unanticipated which will either increase sales or shift their timing, thereby affecting one quarter vs. the other. However, this excludes the overall business plan for the year from being affected. That's why when talking about actual vs. estimate vs. budget, do this for both the sales and royalties to see what impact it has on the overall program.

Roadblocks are another component that the licensee should address to ensure success. The licensee will want to establish a meeting with the DMM (District Marketing Manager) at each retailer as their support is critical to getting the next purchase order, especially if they are having trouble. It is not uncommon for the licensee to come to you and say, "I am aware that you have a relationship with that DMM. Can you help us get them onboard so that we can ensure the success of our program?" Therefore, expect that there will be a multitude of roadblocks to address as you analyze the Quarterly reviews. In addition to roadblocks, other Key Elements are discussed such as: What do those elements to win resemble? How important is one meeting versus another? Is this important product development? What are the specific approvals that are needed to meet a shipment date? This type of material goes into a quarterly review book of the business plan.

In continuation, the **Monthly Business Plan** for sales planning includes:

- Sales calls
- Changes to forecasts
- Challenges
    - Sales
    - Approvals
    - Anything else that impacts the program's success

This is a more detailed program. If we see an Annual Business Plan is primarily strategic and a Quarterly Business Plan as strategic and tactical; the Monthly Business Plan tends to be exclusively tactical.

The Monthly Licensee Dashboard:

- Ties to Annual Business Plan
- Is updated monthly
- Provides key information: budget, forcast, sales/royalties by retailer and product, key dates.

This Monthly Licensee Dashboard is an ongoing plan with updates on a monthly basis. In addition to that, there's probably going to be weekly conversations that are less formal and more informal that will help ensure the success of the program and make sure that everybody is meeting their goals.

Here is a snapshot of the Monthly Licensee Dashboard.

| | | | |
|---|---|---|---|
| Licensee Name | Licensee #1 | Year 2 Licensor Budget: | 3,000,000 |
| Submission Date: | Year 2 | Year 2 Licensee Budget: | 350,000 |
| Royalty Rates (%): | 5, 7.5, 10 | Licensee Contribution: | 12% |
| Minimum Guarantees: | 100,000 | | |
| | | Year 2 Licensor Estimate: | 3,500,000 |
| | | Year 2 Licensee Estimate: | 375,000 |
| | | Licensee Contribution: | 11% |

*PAGE NUMBER*

### Sales & Royalty Summary Goal

| | Year 1 Actual | Year 2 Budget | Estimate | Yr 1 Actual vs. Yr 2 Budget | Yr 2 Budget vs. Estimate |
|---|---|---|---|---|---|
| Sales | 2,500,000 | 3,500,000 | 3,750,000 | 40% | 7% |
| Royalites | 250,000 | 350,000 | 375,000 | 40% | 7% |

### Retailer Summary Goal

| Retailer | Year 1 Sales | Royalties | Year 2 Sales | Royalties | % of Estimate |
|---|---|---|---|---|---|
| Wal-Mart | 658,000 | 65,800 | 770,000 | 77,000 | 21% |
| Target | 475,000 | 47,500 | 573,000 | 57,300 | 15% |
| The Home Depot | 378,000 | 37,800 | 425,000 | 42,500 | 11% |
| Lowe's | 299,000 | 29,900 | 411,000 | 41,100 | 11% |
| SAM's Club | 108,000 | 10,800 | 379,000 | 37,900 | 10% |
| Costco | 107,000 | 10,700 | 368,000 | 36,800 | 10% |
| SEARS | 97,000 | 9,700 | 320,000 | 32,000 | 9% |
| Kmart | 75,000 | 7,500 | 144,000 | 14,400 | 4% |
| Kohl's | 55,000 | 5,500 | 110,000 | 11,000 | 3% |
| Other | 248,000 | 24,800 | 250,000 | 25,000 | 7% |
| Total | 2,500,000 | 250,000 | 3,750,000 | 375,000 | 100% |

### Product Summary Goal

| Product | Year 1 Sales | Royalties | Year 2 Sales | Royalties | % of Estimate |
|---|---|---|---|---|---|
| A | 658,000 | 65,800 | 770,000 | 77,000 | 21% |
| B | 475,000 | 47,500 | 573,000 | 57,300 | 15% |
| C | 378,000 | 37,800 | 425,000 | 42,500 | 11% |
| D | 299,000 | 29,900 | 411,000 | 41,100 | 11% |
| E | 108,000 | 10,800 | 379,000 | 37,900 | 10% |
| F | 107,000 | 10,700 | 368,000 | 36,800 | 10% |
| G | 97,000 | 9,700 | 320,000 | 32,000 | 9% |
| H | 75,000 | 7,500 | 144,000 | 14,400 | 4% |
| | 55,000 | 5,500 | 110,000 | 11,000 | 3% |
| | 248,000 | 24,800 | 250,000 | 25,000 | 7% |
| Total | 2,500,000 | 250,000 | 3,750,000 | 375,000 | 100% |

*Figure 13-2: Monthly Licensee Dashboard*

Let's take a more in-depth look into the Monthly Licensee Dashboard, and you can see it is similar to the Annual Business Plan. The numbers at the top are exactly the same as far as who it is, when it's submitted, the targeted numbers, and the percentages formulated. Although, when you get to the subsection below, on the sales and royalty summary you see the actual numbers and the comparison of actual vs. estimate.

As it relates to the retailer, the same thing is occurring on a monthly basis. The format is exactly the same, but now the licensee will be using actuals vs. estimates on a monthly basis as it relates to sales, royalties, and percentage of the estimate on a full year basis. Take a glance at the left-hand side, at the actual numbers for that particular month. Similarly, again, this is the same type of format used in the Annual Business Plan where there is a drill down on a product basis with the exact relationship of the review vs. the month actuals for the full year. This will allow you as well as the licensee to know if there is a timing issue. Suppose there was a dip in one particular month, but the full year doesn't change. There may have been a missed ship date by a couple of days, but it didn't have any impact on the overall success of the program.

Now that you have a better understanding of the Sale Planning, let's divert attention towards the Marketing Plan. Here the focus is to align the licensee with the licensor as it relates to key marketing initiatives for the coming year. Elements that are important to you, the licensor, will include key changes in packaging, design, brand direction, fashions, and anything that is an exclusive part of the program. At this point, you should bring all the licensees in to talk about their program from a holistic perspective. Questions that you should address are the following:

- What are you doing with marketing initiatives?
- Are there any updates of the branding guidelines?

From this "sit-down", the licensees take that information acquired and then build their business plan. Then they will illustrate what the percentage of the total business they are going to allocate towards marketing. If it's 2 percent or 3 percent of the total it can range from $10,000 to $20,000 to $30,000. If this amount is multiplied by 10 or 20 licensees in your program, you can conclude you have a significant marketing budget. This helps you to compare these marketing budget numbers against your core business and see what the overall impact could be in strengthening the brand and helping to ensure the success of the program across all categories. Any key relationships are discussed here as well because it is important to know how you and the licensee cooperate as it relates to advertising buys, PR initiatives, and any other elements in the marketing mix to ensure the success of both the category and the overall brand on an annual basis.

The last piece of the business plan is **Quality and Compliance Management.** It is vital at this stage to review the contract compliance and what is taking place with the contract. As the licensor, you want to verify the licensee is actually complying with all of the guidelines provided in the contract. That includes orientation, annual business plan reviews, and routine audits.

Routine audits are important as you move forward with your licensing program. Sometimes issues are discovered that were not intentionally done incorrectly by the licensee such as a process oversight or information that has to be shared that would have helped the overall program improve and be more successful. Therefore, a routine audit should not be something the licensee should be concerned about if they are following the guidelines of the contract. Finally, we get to Product Approvals and Financial Reporting. Are those things being complied with as it relates to the contract? If yes, the success of the program is going to follow.

From the Quality Insurance perspective, you are going to make routine site visits? These visits take place at the offices of the licensee or at their manufacturing facilities to make sure everything is in compliance, just as you would do so if that particular entity was part of your own company. This is not anything that is out of the norm. You should also examine the supplier and manufacturer approvals to make sure that the product that is being provided by the suppliers and the manufacturers are meeting their own approval process without any gaps, slip-ups, or problems. Finally, there is a QA report card that's taken to show where the licensee measures against a list of core criteria to assess the overall success of the quality of the program. This is foundationally important to make sure that products in the marketplace are meeting and exceeding standards.

Now you can see the whole summarized process from starting with Step 1, which was Identifying Where to Play all the way through to Step 8 which is Establish Business Plan. This completes the process 8-Step Brand Licensing Process, and now you can be assured that your product is in the marketplace and its selling to the consumers. Because of all the work you have done as a brand owner up to this point, the likelihood of the success of these product's sales is very high.

Congratulations!!! You to have completed this series of *Breakthrough Licensing: A Disciplined Path To Profitable Brand Extensions.* It is normal at this point to feel a little bit overwhelmed due to the depth of the information provided, but rest assured we are here and we are going to continue to provide you with necessary tools to ensure your continued success. We are excited that you are a part of this program and are excited that you have gone through these steps. You should feel justifiably proud! If you would like more information about how to continue to grow your business visit petecanalichio.com. We look forward to hearing about the successfully commercialize your own program.

# References

1. Forbes Corporate Communications Forbes Staff. (2017). *Forbes Releases Seventh Annual World's Most Valuble Brands.* Retrieved from http://www.forbes. com/sites /forbespr/2017/05/23/ forbes-releases-seventh-annual-worlds-most- valuable- brands-list/#1a18b3e75b55

2. Kotler, P., & Armstrong, G. (2018). *Principles of Marketing* (17thed.). Hoboken: Pearson Higher Education.

3. LIMA. (2017). *Global Retail and Other Revenues Generated by Licensed Goods and Services Grew 3.3% to 271.6B in 2017.* Retrieved from http://www. licensing.org/inside-licensing/global-retail-and-other-revenues- generated-by-licensed- goods-and-services-grew-3-3-to-271-6b-in-2017/

4. Licensing Industry Merchandisers Association (LIMA). Retrieved from http://www.licensing.org

5. Manton, Steven. (2005). *Integrated Intel lectual Assets Management.* Gower Publishing, LTD.

6. Statista. (2017). *The 100 Largest Companies in the World by Market Valuein 2017.* Retrived from http://www.statista.com/statistics/263264/ top-companies-in- the-world-by- market-value/

# More Books by Pete Canalichio

### 35 Case Studies Of Brands That Successfully Entered New Categories

With 35 case studies all in one place you'll save hours of searching on Google. With analysis by brand licensing expert Pete Canalichio, you'll get a better understanding of licensing strategies and the way brands in other industries have succeeded.

### Brand Licensing Agreement Templates

Fill-in-the-blank templates modeled after Coca-Cola and Newell-Rubbermaid's standard licensing contracts. Includes guide with call-outs explaining the meaning and benefits of each contract clause.

### Is You're Brand Ready To Stretch Into New Categories

Use a proven scoring system to decide if your brand is ready to stretch, avoid catastrophic failures, know how to get your brand ready to expand and extend if it scores badly and build on your brand's strengths if it scores well.

Printed in Great Britain
by Amazon

26455857R00089